Copyright ©

ISBN 978-0-915545-08-7
First Printing 1986
Revised Printing 2013

Printed in the United States of America
All Rights Reserved!

Published by
Stanley R. Abbott Ministries, Inc.
P.O. Box 533
McRae, Georgia 31055
U.S.A.

Temple of Glory

PREFACE

Jesus said the ones who believe on Him will do the works He did. Yet today when we look at the church, we see individual Christians en masse who are defeated and unfulfilled. Not only are we not doing the works of Jesus, we suffer emotional problems, financial woes, health troubles, and relationship breakdowns at an alarming rate. Rather than looking like Christ in our works, it is hard to tell most Christians from unbelievers. Something is very, very wrong.

Where is the breakdown? What is the solution? Doesn't God have a purpose and a plan for us? Our God is good, His mercy endures forever, and He loves you and me. The sacrifice of His Son, Jesus, on the cross demonstrated this love. He is a Father who wants the very best for His children. He has planned carefully for our lives. However, until we learn what His plan is and understand His purpose, we will never become who He wants us to be. The intent for this book is to explore God's plan and purpose for us and to find His way to achieve His results for our lives.

Temple of Glory

TABLE OF CONTENTS

Part One
God's Plan For Man

Chapter One
Pre-Creation Realities — 1

Chapter Two
Love, Sonship, and Dominion — 17

Chapter Three
The Commission of Jesus — 35

Part Two
God's Method to Achieve His Plan

Chapter Four
Supernatural Personnel — 53

Chapter Five
The Calling — 67

Chapter Six
Receiving A Ministry Gift — 81

Chapter Seven
Defining The Gifts   95

Chapter Eight
Interrelationship Between Ministry Gifts   141

Chapter Nine
Ministry Relationship With The Saints   161

Chapter Ten
Parent-Child Relationship Model   173

Conclusion

Summary   201

Chapter One

PRE-CREATION REALITIES

"In the beginning God created the heavens and the earth." **Genesis 1:1**

Moses is telling us the first four days were devoted to the creation of the heavens and the earth. Isaiah adds

"For thus says the Lord, Who created the heavens, Who is God, Who formed the earth and made it, Who has established it, Who did not create it in vain, Who formed it to be inhabited..." **Isaiah 45:18**

Creation was formed to be inhabited.

God who created the heavens and the earth also created the earth's inhabitants. These inhabitants were fish of the sea, fowl of the air, and beasts of the field. However, God's plan called for more than fish, fowl, and beasts to inhabit the earth. He had in His plan a very special creation, one to be created in His own image. This creation was to be called man. God made man in His own image

"You have made him a little lower than the angels and You have crowned him with glory and honour."
Psalms 8:5

Man was the most special of all of creation because it was unto man the Lord God gave dominion of creation. God chose man to rule over the fish of the sea, the fowl of the air, the beasts of the field, and over all the earth. Because the creator Himself gave such dominion to man, creation had to obey. Creation had no choice but to do what the Creator said. The Creator said man had dominion over creation, therefore creation had to do what man said.

MAN GIVEN FREEDOM

Man was different. He was unique among all creation. God gave man freedom of choice. There is no one particular scripture which tells us exactly why God gave man this freedom, but there is a theme throughout the entire Bible which helps us understand why. Paul's letters to the churches at Rome and Corinth help us begin to answer this question.

By inspiration of the Holy Spirit Paul compared Christ with Adam. Paul pointed out it was by the man Adam that sin and death came into the world and, so, it must be by the man Jesus that righteousness and life be restored. Paul even went so far with the comparison to call Jesus the last Adam. Because the Holy Spirit inspired this type of comparison, there must be similarities in the way God saw both Jesus and Adam. Two of the most significant pieces of information regarding this comparison are found in the gospel of John,

Pre-Creation Realities

"For God so loved the world, that He gave His only begotten Son, that whoever believes in Him should not perish, but have everlasting life." **John 3:16**

The two pieces of information to consider are:

"...love..." and *"...sonship..."*

MOTIVATED BY LOVE

John told us *"...the Father loves the Son..."* **John 3:35**. In **John 3:16** Jesus Himself told us how *"...God loved the world..."*. It was God's love relationship with man that motivated Him to send Jesus into the world as man's redeemer. Adam was part of the world, so it is without question that God loved Adam.

If God loved Adam, we can assume God desired for Adam to love Him back. A love relationship should be reciprocal, not out of necessity but out of desire. It would not have been a reciprocal love relationship if Adam would not have had a choice in the matter. God gave Adam freedom to choose whether or not he would love Him. If Adam chose to love God, it would be a true love from the heart, and not out of necessity. This is the basis for real love: love from the heart, not out of necessity. God, Himself, gave us this example by showing us

"But God, who is rich in mercy, because of His great love with which He loved us, even when we were dead in trespasses..." **Ephesians 2:4,5**

God did not love us because He had to or because of our good works. Rather, He loved us from His heart even though we were dead in our sins. This is the kind of love God wants from us: ***love freely given from the heart***. This kind of love can only come from one who is free to choose to give it or not to give it.

SONSHIP

The second piece of information to consider from ***John 3:16*** regarding Adam's freedom of choice is *"...sonship..."* We are looking at the comparison between Jesus and Adam. How God saw Jesus as the last Adam would be similar to the way He saw the first Adam.

When God sent Jesus into the earth, He did not have to send Him as His son. He could have sent Him as just another creation man. It was His will that Jesus come into the earth as His son. God had a reason for sending Jesus as His son.

So, too, Jesus' redemption did not have to make us sons of God. It could have just made us servants of God. But it was the will of God that Jesus' redemption make us ***"...sons..."***

> *"...as many as received Him (Jesus), to them He gave the right to become the **children** of God, to those who believe in His name: who were born not of blood, nor of the will of the flesh, nor of the will of man, but of God..."*
> ***John 1:12,13***

There was a reason why God made the believers sons.

Pre-Creation Realities

It was the will of God to send Jesus into the earth as His son and to make the believers sons. The same Greek word translated *"...will..."* can also be translated *"...desire..."* Therefore, because it was the *"...will..."* of God to make Jesus and the believers sons, then it was also His *"...desire..."* for us to be sons. Because it was the *will* and *desire* of God for us to be sons, it is reasonable to conclude that God wanted to relate to us as **Father**.

A servant has no choice but to serve his master. A son can choose to serve his father or not, as we see in the case of the prodigal son in **Luke 15:11-32**. If Adam had been created as a servant without freedom of choice, he could not have demonstrated sonship to God. Then, God could not have enjoyed a **Father-son** relationship. Instead, man would have simply been a servant bound to do the will of his **creator**. However, as a free man Adam would have freedom to choose.

One of the main reasons God sent Jesus into the earth as His son and made believers sons was to fulfill His Fatherhood desires. Our God is the

"...Father of lights, with whom there is no variation or shadow of turning..." **James 1:17**

In other words, God is constant and unchanging. If God had a desire to relate to man as Father through Jesus and the believers, then that desire always existed in God. He changes not.

God reveals Himself to man in different ways, but He changes not. His will and desire remain constant. His desire to be Father to man existed even before He created Adam. Surely God wanted to have this Father - son relationship with Adam as His first man. He created Adam with freedom of choice rather than as a servant without choice in order to have this relationship.

God created Adam with freedom to choose in order to have man love and serve Him out of the abundance of his heart. God wanted man to love and serve Him because he wanted to, not because he had to. This was a dangerous thing for God to do because if man had the freedom to choose to love and serve God, then man might choose *not* to love and serve God. However, God was willing to take the risk!

KNOWLEDGE OF TIME

Man can look back in time through recorded history and know what free choice the man Adam made. Time as we know it for past, present, and future events is determined by the movement of the planets around the sun. We can pinpoint past events by accurately calculating the already completed movements of the planets. We know present events in the time according to the planets' current movements. We are restrained from knowing the future as natural men because of our existence within the natural physical universe. The planets have not yet moved around the sun in the course they will take tomorrow. Therefore, tomorrow's events have not yet occurred. As natural men our knowledge of future events is limited to only proposals and projections because of these restrictions of the laws of the natural physical universe.

Pre-Creation Realities

UNRESTRICTED KNOWLEDGE

God who created the natural physical universe is not restricted by His own creation. He is greater than the laws He set in motion. The psalmist said,

> *"Great is our Lord, and mighty in power: His understanding is infinite."* **Psalms 147:5**

The prophet Isaiah said,

> *"Have you not known? Have you not heard? The everlasting God, the Lord, the Creator of the ends of the earth, neither faints nor is weary? His understanding is unsearchable."* **Isaiah 40:28**

What God knows is infinite, without restrictions. That includes His knowledge of His creation. God sees backward and forward in time in the natural physical universe. He is not restricted by the movement of the planets He created. He knows what is going to happen tomorrow. That does not mean He is making things happen tomorrow in some puppet-type of predestination. No, our omniscient God is simply greater than natural time. He knows all things, even the future.

While you and I can only look back in the past through history to know what has already occurred, God can look forward into the future to know what will occur. He is not ordering the future but He knows the future. We look back to see what Adam did, but God looked forward to see what Adam was going to do. We know by Moses' record of history that

Adam chose of his own free will to follow the will or desire of Satan *(See **Genesis Chapter 3**)*. Paul told us...

> "...*that to whom you present yourselves slaves to obey, you are that one's slaves whom ye obey...*" **Romans 6:16**

Adam became the servant of Satan, and Satan took his place as master of creation. This is how sin and death entered the world: **through Adam's free-will choice to serve Satan.**

God did not make Adam choose sin and death. God gave Adam freedom of choice, and Adam chose of his own free will. Because God knows the future, He knew what Adam was going to choose. God also knew Adam's choice would cause sin and death to pass upon all men of the earth because of Satan's lordship over creation *(See **Romans 5:12-21**)*. This meant man must have help to be free from the bondage of an evil master in order to love and serve God as sons.

A MYSTERY FOREORDAINED

Even before the world began God made provision for man's redemption.

> "...*knowing that ye were not redeemed with corruptible things, like silver or gold, from your aimless conduct received by tradition from your fathers, but with the precious blood of Christ, as of a lamb without blemish and without spot, He indeed was foreordained before the foundation of the world, but was manifest in these last times for you...*" **I Peter 1:18-20**

Pre-Creation Realities

Paul said it this way,

> "...God, who has saved us and called us with a holy calling, not according to our works, but according to his own purpose and grace which was given to us in Christ Jesus before time began, but now has been revealed by the appearing of our Savior Jesus Christ, who has abolished death, and brought life and immortality to light through the gospel." **II Timothy 1:9,10**

God's plan, which He conceived before the world began, was far more comprehensive than just redemption from death. His plan was complete for man and the earth throughout eternity. It was so powerful and full of life that He conceived it in secrecy and clothed it in mystery.

Throughout the history of man, up to the Church Age, God only revealed glimpses of His plan to man. No one knew the secret of the mystery because it was not God's will or time to reveal it to anyone. Paul told us by inspiration of the Holy Spirit why the mysterious plan was kept such a secret. He said,

> "...We speak the wisdom of God in a mystery, the hidden wisdom which God ordained before the ages for our glory, which none of the rulers of this age knew; for had they known, they would not have crucified the Lord of glory..." **I Corinthians 2:7,8**

God did not want to jeopardize His plan so He just kept the secret of the plan hidden in a mystery.

REVELATION OF THE MYSTERY

In the close of his letter to the Church at Rome the apostle Paul commended the saints to the grace of our Lord Jesus Christ. Then he wrote a very interesting line,

> *"Now to him Who is able to establish you according to my gospel and the preaching of Jesus Christ, according to the revelation of the mystery kept secret since the world began..."* **Romans 16:25**

We know it is God who establishes the believer. Notice how God establishes the believers,

> *"...according to my gospel, and the preaching of Jesus Christ, according to the revelation of the mystery kept secret since the world began..."*

Revelation of the mystery has establishing power in the life of a believer.

If it is important enough to help establish me, then certainly I want to understand God's mystery. I want to be established as a believer. Therefore, I must have a revelation of this mystery. A revelation of the mystery means understanding of the mystery has to be revealed to me.

The mystery was kept secret until after the crucifixion of the Lord of glory as we saw in ***I Corinthians 2:8***. Search for understanding must begin in the New Testament. Jesus first used the term *"...mystery..."* when He told the parable of the sower. He said to the disciples,

Pre-Creation Realities

> *"...it has been given to you know the mysteries of the kingdom of heaven (God)..."*
> **Matthew 13:11, Mark 4:11, and Luke 8:10**

Throughout both the Old and New Testaments it is clear there are secret things of God which no man can understand unless God, Himself, reveal them. As Moses wrote,

> *"The secret things belong to the Lord our God, but those things which are revealed belong to us and to our children forever..."* **Deuteronomy 29:29**

Thank God it is given unto you and me to know the *"...mysteries..."* of the kingdom.

MYSTERIES OF THE KINGDOM

In the parallel accounts of the parable of the sower, the term *"...mystery..."* is used in both singular and plural senses. Matthew and Luke recorded Jesus as saying *"...mysteries of the kingdom..."* Mark records *"...mystery of the kingdom..."* We can see by the use of the term *"...mysteries..."* there is more than one mystery in the kingdom of God. We understand this by looking at what Jesus *"...revealed..."* to the disciples about the parable of the sower. The parable remained a mystery to some but Jesus gave understanding to His disciples. He revealed the *"...mystery..."* of the parable.

The parable hid a secret of the kingdom of God. Therefore, when Jesus revealed the mystery of the parable, He was revealing a secret of the kingdom. Because Jesus taught many parables, in this sense, there are many mysteries of the kingdom. Every teaching Jesus taught was like an individual brush stroke on a canvas working toward revelation of *"...one..."* complete picture. This complete picture, even though containing many individual mysteries, is the *"...mystery..."* of God's will for man and the earth which God conceived before the world was formed.

Simon Peter had a revelation of one of these individual mysteries when he identified Jesus as, *"...the Christ, the Son of the living God..."* Jesus then said unto Peter,

> *"Blessed are you, Simon Bar-Jonah: for flesh and blood has not revealed this to you, but my Father who is in heaven..."* **Matthew 16:16,17**

This revelation from God was only part of the great mystery hidden by God. Even this part of the mystery that Jesus is the Christ, the Messiah, the Savior, the Lamb of God which takes away the sin of the world was conceived before the foundation of the world as we have already seen.

> *"...knowing that you were not redeemed with corruptible things, like silver or gold, from your aimless conduct received by tradition from your fathers, but with the precious blood of Christ, as of a lamb without blemish and without spot, He indeed was foreordained before the foundation of the world, but was manifest in these last times for you..."* **I Peter 1:18-20**

Pre-Creation Realities

PAUL'S REVELATION

Paul as an apostle had great revelation concerning God's mystery. He taught on the mystery because he knew it was foundational for the Church and for the life of every Christian. Paul begins to unfold the mystery as he explains how God had,

> "...made known to us the mystery of His will, according to His good pleasure which He purposed in Himself, that in the fullness of the times He might gather together in one all things in Christ, both which are in heaven, and which are on earth in Him...And He has put all things under His feet, and gave Him to be head over all things to the church, which is His body, the fullness of Him who fills all in all..." **Ephesians 1:9-23**

Within this passage of scripture we get our first glimpse of "...the mystery..." God's will is that He might gather together in one all things in Christ. This does not make the mystery plain to us. Paul gives us further information on the mystery later in his letter to the Ephesians. He began to teach on submission in the marriage relationship between husband and wife.

> "...For we are members of His body, of His flesh, and of His bones. For this reason a man shall leave his father and mother and be joined to his wife, and the two shall become one flesh. This is a great mystery, but I speak concerning Christ and the church..."
> **Ephesians 5:30-33**

The mystery becomes a little clearer here that "...all things gathered together in one in Christ..." is referring to Christ and the Church becoming one like a husband and a wife become one flesh. In his letter to the Church at Colosse Paul speaks again about the mystery. He says,

> "...of which I became a minister, according to the stewardship from God which was given to me for you, to fulfill the Word of God, the mystery which has been hidden from ages and from generations, but now has been revealed to His saints. To them God willed to make known what are the riches of the glory of this mystery among the Gentiles: which is Christ in you, the hope of glory..."
> **Colossians 1:25-29**

UNDERSTANDING THE MYSTERY

Now we understand a larger percentage of the hidden wisdom of God conceived in secrecy from the foundation of the world. The great master plan of God which had been clothed in mystery throughout the ages was not just that God would send His Word to be made flesh and dwell among man as Christ Jesus. That was only part of the plan. The balance of the mystery was that God would send His Word as Christ to dwell in the heart of every man who believed on Jesus and together all believers would actually be the body of Christ.

Imagine the terror that mystery revealed must strike in the heart of the devil. It was God living in flesh *(in the person of Jesus the Christ)* who defeated Satan, destroying his works and making a show of them openly, triumphing over him in it. Now, God in His infinite wisdom, has devised a plan so that He will not be in just one man, Christ Jesus, but God as Christ Jesus will be in all men who will believe on Him!

Pre-Creation Realities

Jesus identifies this type of relationship with the Father as the basis for *"...all..."* He did while He walked on the earth.

> *"...Do you not believe that I am in the Father, and the Father in Me? The words that I speak to you I do not speak on My own authority; but the Father who dwells in Me does the works. Believe Me that I am in the Father, and the Father in Me, or else believe Me for the sake of the works themselves..."* **John 14:10,11**

It was God in the man Jesus who actually did the supernatural works through Jesus.

Immediately following this statement about the Father dwelling in Christ doing the works through Him, Jesus said,

> *"Most assuredly, I say to you, he who believes in Me, the works that I do he will do also; and greater works than these he will do; because I go to My Father..."*
> **John 14:12**

It is when we believe on Jesus that God comes to dwell in us: **That is the Master Plan;** the great mystery hidden from ages and generations. The mystery which if the princes of this world had known they would not have crucified the Lord of glory. Because with Jesus' crucifixion we were made ready to be a part of God's Master Plan. Without the crucifixion God's plan could not have been fulfilled. Now, because of the crucifixion, every believer as a child of God has God living on the inside of them.

Just as God-in-man was the basis for Jesus' earthly ministry, God-in-man is the basis for every believer being able to walk supernaturally doing the works of Jesus here on the earth!

God in us, the hope of Glory!

Chapter Two

LOVE, SONSHIP, & DOMINION

Now that we have discovered *what* the hidden wisdom of God is, which had been hidden in a mystery from ages and generations, we must understand *why* God conceived such a plan. We also need to consider *how* the plan was to become operational in the earth.

To ask the question why God conceived His plan would be the same thing as to search for the purpose of His plan. We have already seen the simplicity of God's plan: ***God planned to unite with man in a relationship so that He and man would become one.***

This plan was progressively unfolded to us as Paul told us God's will was to gather together in one all things in Christ. More clearly, Paul told us that all things gathered together in one is the Church joined to Christ just as a man joined unto his wife is one flesh. Finally, Paul spoke plainly of the plan which is Christ in Christians, the hope of glory. God and man united as one in the earth.

THE PURPOSE OF GOD'S PLAN

In our search for the purpose of God's plan for man in these last days, we must reflect back on God's purpose for man in the beginning. We have seen that God created Adam out of a desire to walk with man as Father. God created man in His own image and gave him dominion over all the earth. If God gave man dominion of the earth, then we can be confident in making the statement, "It was God's will and desire for man to have dominion of the earth". God created man to walk with Him in a *Father-son* relationship of love with man ruling over the works of the Father's hands. Imagine, **mankind** created to walk with God as ruler over creation!

Because this was God's purpose for **mankind** in the beginning, then this would also be God's purpose for **mankind** today. What God purposes in His heart He cannot change. God wants to walk with **mankind** in a *Father-son* relationship of love with man ruling over creation. We need confirmation of this purpose in the Word.

LOVE

We see these three purposes of love, sonship, and dominion spoken of in the New Testament over and over again. John wrote of the love relationship between God and man.

> "Beloved, let us love one another, for love is of God; and everyone that loves is born of God and knows God. He who does not love does not know God, for God is love. In this the love of God was manifested toward us, that God has sent His only begotten Son into the world, that we might live through Him. In this is love, not that we loved God, but that He loved us, and sent His Son to be the propitiation for our sins. Beloved, if God so loved us, we also ought to love one another. No one has seen God at any time. If we love one another, God abides in

> us, and His love has been perfected in us...We love Him, because He first loved us. If someone says, I love God, and hates his brother, he is a liar; for he who does not love his brother whom he has seen, how can he love God whom he hath not seen? And this commandment we have from Him: that he who loves God must love his brother also." ***I John 4:7-21***

The love relationship God has ordained for man is so powerful it extends beyond man's love for God. It reaches out from man to man. This incredible ability God has given a new creation man to love is based on two facts:

1. *God has first loved man.*

2. *God has actually come to dwell in the heart of every man who believes.*

God is love! Therefore, supernatural love dwells in every Christian. God's purpose for man to be a love-creature was fulfilled by God uniting with man.

SONSHIP

John also wrote of sonship.

> "Behold, what manner of love the Father has bestowed on us, that we would be called the children of God! Therefore the world does not know us, because it did not know Him. Beloved, now we are the children of God, and it has not yet been revealed what we shall be, but we know that when He is revealed, we shall be like Him; for we shall see Him as he is..." ***I John 3:1,2***

Temple of Glory

It was the love of the Father that motivated Him to make us sons. Again John wrote of God's will to make us sons.

> "...*as many as received Him, to them He gave the right to become the children of God, to those who believe in His name: who were born, not of blood, nor of the will of the flesh, nor of the will of man, but of God...*"
> **John 1:12,13**

It was God's will to make us sons because of His love for us!

DOMINION

Jesus, Himself, spoke of the dominion in which man was to walk. He said,

> "*Most assuredly, I say to you, he who believes in Me, the works that I do he will do also; and greater works than these he will do; because I go to My Father.*"
> **John 14:12**

From the mouth of Jesus Himself it is established that believers are to do the works of Jesus.

Jesus' works were works of dominion demonstrated in both the spiritual realm and the natural physical universe. He had authority over evil spirits, and He had authority over the wind and the sea. Jesus called dead men's spirits back into their bodies to live again, and He multiplied five loaves and two fish to feed five thousand. Jesus was able to produce these supernatural works of dominion because of the Father in Him. So, too, it is because of Christ in us that He expects us to do these same works which He did:

*...works of dominion in both the
spiritual and natural realms.*

All three of these, love, sonship, and dominion work together. Those who are expected to do the works of Jesus are believers. John told us that believers have been made to be sons of God. John also told us God made us sons because of His love for us. We have dominion as sons of God and we are sons because of His love. Seeing God's purpose for man in these last days helps us understand why God conceived His plan which He conceived before the foundation of the world: ***in order to bring man back to a place of sonship, through love, having dominion over creation.***

PLAN IN OPERATION

Now, what about the plan becoming operational in the earth? The plan had to be developed in stages of which there are many. Each stage had its part to play in bringing the ultimate plan into operation in the earth.

➤ There were the covenant relationships between God and man and the giving of the law as preparation for the coming Christ. As Paul wrote,

> *"...the law was our tutor to bring us unto Christ,
> that we might be justified by faith..."* **Galatians 3:24**

➤ There was the virgin birth which could only occur at a prescribed time according to God's determination.

Temple of Glory

> *"...when the fullness of time had come, God sent forth His Son, born of a woman, born under the law, to redeem those who were under the law, that we might receive the adoption as sons..."*
> **Galatians 4:4,5**

- There was Jesus' earthly life and ministry which destroyed the works of the devil providing redemption for man.

- There was the new birth or salvation by grace through faith which made many sons of God.

There were so many parts of the plan, so many fine details, I suppose that even the world itself could not contain the books which could be written about them.

God's plan is being fulfilled daily as men and women, boys and girls all over the world are being born again with God coming to live inside them. Every person who is born again is a part of God's plan in fulfillment. God's plan is to unite with man in a relationship so that He and man become one on the earth.

This new birth part of the plan is not the end in itself. It is a means unto the end. The purpose of God's plan was not just to have God united with man, but rather to bring man to a place of sonship, through love, to have dominion over creation. That is why evangelism is not all there is to the great commission. Evangelism is only part of the great commission.

The goal of evangelism is to get a person born again. When a person is born again, part of the new birth process is

God coming to dwell within the new believer. We have already seen God dwelling in man is not the end of the master plan. That is really just the beginning. If we evangelized the whole world, we would be only at the initial stages of fulfilling God's plan.

God has planned to come dwell in man so He and man, united in the earth as Father and son, might do the works of Jesus. There are millions of people who are in bondage to the works of Satan. God's plan for those in bondage to be set free is for every person who has Christ in them to destroy the works of the devil in the lives of whomsoever will.

Evangelizing a person, getting them born again to have God come dwell on the inside of them, is only a beginning. When a person is first born again, he is a *"...babe-in-Christ..."* without understanding who God really is in them or who they are in Christ. They must be taught so they can become mature in Christ. They must learn that eternal life is not just quantity of days but rather as Jesus said,

> *"...this is life eternal, that they might know You, the only true God, and Jesus Christ, whom You have sent..."*
> **John 17:3**

In order to help babes in Christ reach a place of maturity to be able to do the works of Jesus, they must be taught to know the Father and the Son. This intimate knowledge is not knowing about, but rather relationship with, the Father and the Son. The greater the knowledge of God we have, the higher the level of His kind of life will be manifest in us. Therefore, teaching is as a vital part of the great commission as is evangelism.

Evangelism and teaching are not all there is to the great commission either. While meditating on these things one day, the Lord began to speak to me. He said,

"Son, there are three basic requirements for the Church to be successful in the earth:

1. You must understand what you have been commissioned to do.

2. You must have supernatural personnel with divinely given abilities.

3. And you must have adequate provision of material and funds."

Then, the Lord explained there were three men in the Bible who had parallel commissions. He said He would show me these three requirements for success in their lives. The first man was Moses.

MOSES' COMMISSION

After Jehovah delivered the Israelites from the house of bondage in Egypt, He started moving them toward the promised land. In transit He gave them ten commandments, diverse laws, and ordinances to help their lives. He also desired to dwell among them. They were spiritually dead so He could not dwell in them as He does in us today. It was not time for Christ to be given so He gave Moses the commission to,

> "...make Me a sanctuary, that I may dwell among them. According to all that I show you, the pattern of the tabernacle and the pattern of all the furnishings, just so shall ye make it..." **Exodus 25:8,9**

This was the *first requirement* for Moses to be able to successfully fulfill what God had asked him to do. **Moses had to understand his commission.** God gave Moses the commission together with specific pattern and details. Moses knew exactly what to do.

We know from **Hebrews 8:1-5** and **Hebrews 9:19-24** the tabernacle Moses was commissioned to build was patterned after the true tabernacle which the Lord pitched and not man: *the tabernacle in heaven.* Can you imagine the Lord showing Moses a pattern of heavenly things and expecting Moses to convert what he saw into earthly copies? This would be impossible for natural man with only natural abilities. This leads to our *second requirement* for success: **supernatural personnel with divinely given abilities.**

God spoke to Moses, saying,

> "Then the Lord spoke to Moses saying: See, I have called by name Bezaleel the son of Uri, the son of Hur, of the tribe of Judah. And I have filled him with the Spirit of God, in wisdom, and in understanding, and in knowledge, and in all manner of workmanship, to design artistic works, to work in gold, in silver, in bronze, in cutting jewels for setting, in carving wood, and to work in all manner of workmanship. And I, indeed, I have appointed with him Aholiab, the son of Ahisamach, of the tribe of Dan: and I have put wisdom in the hearts of all the gifted artisans, that they may make all that I have commanded you." **Exodus 31:1-6**

Temple of Glory

God who gave the commission also provided the supernatural personnel and abilities so the commission could be fulfilled.

Our third requirement for success is different. God was responsible for the first two requirements. He instructs Moses about the third requirement of adequate provision of material and funds,

> "Speak unto the children of Israel, that they bring Me an offering, *from everyone who gives it willingly with his heart ye shall take My offering.* And this is the offering you shall take of them; gold, silver, and bronze, blue, purple, scarlet thread, fine linen, and goats' hair, rams' skins dyed red, badgers' skins, and acacia wood; oil for the light, and spices for the anointing oil and for the sweet incense; onyx stones, and stones to be set in the ephod, and in the breastplate..." **Exodus 25:2-7**

God commissioned man to do a work in the earth. God provided supernatural personnel to do the work. But God expected man to supply the materials and funds for His work to be done. Imagine that!

Notice He said it was to be a free will offering; every man that giveth it willingly with his heart. Look at the results!

> "...The people bring much more than enough for the service of the work which the Lord commanded us to do. So Moses gave commandment, and they caused it to be proclaimed throughout the camp, saying, Let neither man nor woman do any more work for the offering of the sanctuary. And the people were restrained from bringing. For the material they had was sufficient for all the work to be done, indeed too much." **Exodus 36:5-6**

What made these spiritually dead men willing to give so liberally from the heart? Two things caused this to happen:

1. ***They had been supernaturally blessed with the wealth of Egypt.** (See Exodus 3:19-22)*

2. ***They understood the commission.***

They knew when the tabernacle was completed God would dwell among them. They were eager to have this happen because they had just been delivered from the most powerful nation on the face of the earth by the hand of God. They could only imagine what it would mean to have this same God actually dwelling among them as their God! God also gave them another more specific reason for the tabernacle,

> *"This shall be a continual burnt offering throughout your generations at the door of the tabernacle of meeting before the Lord, where I will meet you (Moses) to speak with you. And there I will meet with the children of Israel..."* **Exodus 29:42,43**

It is easy to see why they were eager to complete the tabernacle. When the tabernacle was completed, they would be able to meet with God Himself as He dwelt among them!

We see the three requirements for success met.

➤ *Moses as the leader over Israel understood his commission from God to build the tabernacle of the Lord in the earth.*

- *God gave Moses the supernatural personnel to fulfill the commission.*

- *Man provided the materials and funds for God's work to be done.*

The three requirements for success were met and success was attained: The tabernacle was built and God dwelt among the people speaking to Moses and meeting with the children of Israel at the door of the tabernacle. Our omnipresent God manifested His life, nature, and glory to the Israelites through this physical dwelling place.

SOLOMON'S COMMISSION

Our second man with a parallel commission to Moses was Solomon. King David assembled all the leaders of Israel together in Jerusalem and said,

> *"As for me, I had in my heart to build a house of rest for the ark of the covenant of the Lord, and for the footstool of our God, and had made ready for the building: But God said to me, you shall not build a house for My name, because you have been a man of war, and have shed blood."* ***I Chronicles 28:2,3***

David was about to enter into the commission to build the Temple of the Lord. God said no. God said to David,

> *"It is your son Solomon who shall build My house and my courts; for I have chosen him..."* ***I Chronicles 28:6***

> *"Then David gave his son Solomon the plans for the vestibule, its houses, its treasuries, its upper chambers, its inner chambers, and the place of the mercy seat; and the plans for all that he had by the Spirit...All this, said David, the Lord made me understand in writing, by His hand upon me, all the works of these plans."*
> ***I Chronicles 28:11,12,19***

Here is our first requirement for success: ***Solomon understanding the commission from God.***

After David had conveyed the commission with all of its details from the Lord unto Solomon, he began to exhort Solomon for the task that lay ahead. He said,

> *"...Be strong and of a good courage, and do it; do not fear nor be dismayed, for the Lord God, my God, will be with you. He wll not leave you nor forsake you, until you have finished all the work for the service of the house of the Lord. Here are the divisions of the priests and the Levites for all the service of the house of God: and every willing craftsman will be with you for all manner of workmanship, for every kind of service: also the leaders and all the people will be completely at your command."* ***I Chronicles 28:20,21***

The range of help Solomon was to have in order to see his commission fulfilled was very broad, from priest to willing skillful men, to every person of the nation of Israel. Every person of Israel was a part of God's supernaturally chosen and delivered people and they were *"...all..."* to be at Solomon's command. The second requirement for success seems to be more comprehensively met in the case of Solomon than for Moses. Even so, supernatural personnel were added by God for both men to see their commissions fulfilled.

Temple of Glory

Then King David and the people of Israel made offerings of gold, silver, brass, iron, and precious stones for the work of the Lord to be done in the earth.

> *"Then the people rejoiced, for they had offered willingly, because with a loyal heart they had offered willingly to the Lord; and King David also rejoiced greatly."*
> *I Chronicles 29:9*

It is wonderful to see such rejoicing over giving, especially from spiritually dead men. They gave with the same enthusiasm the children of Israel gave for the building of the tabernacle for Moses' commission to be fulfilled. The two motivating factors were the same: **The people had been supernaturally blessed with wealth and they understood fulfillment of the commission would bring manifestation of the life of God into their midst.** What marvelous reasons to give from the heart!

Once again our three requirements for success have been met; this time in order to bring success to Solomon and Israel.

God provided the commission and the supernatural personnel, but the people supplied the materials and funds.

The Temple of the Lord was able to be built according to the Lord's will and desire.

> *"Then the Lord appeared to Solomon by night, and said to him: "I have heard your prayer, and have chosen this*

place for Myself as a house of sacrifice...Now My eyes will be open and My ears attentive to prayer made in this place. For now I have chosen and sanctified this house, that My name may be there forever; and My eyes and My heart will be there perpetually."

II Chronicles 7:12-16

Just think of what that meant, God dwelling in their midst. Too often today Christians have become calloused to God's reality among us. We say with the greatest of ease, "God lives in me." That does not bring the same reverential fear to us as it did to the Israelites. This is because of a lack of understanding of the *"...reality..."* of God's presence in us.

The old covenant people of God had an external relationship with God through the natural man because they were spiritually dead. You and I have a far greater internal relationship with Him through the spirit man now that we are spiritually alive. Because our spiritual senses are not as highly developed as the Israelites' natural senses, they saw the presence of God on the outside better than we do on the inside. They felt and heard His presence externally with greater awareness than we do internally. However, we are the ones who have received the new covenant established on better promises. We have already seen it was the Father in Christ who did the works Jesus did. If we truly understood the reality of God in us, we, too, would be walking like Jesus. What a glorious thing the Israelites had; God in the temple.

***How much more glorious a thing we have,
God in us as His temple!***

I was excited to see the three requirements for success illustrated so fully in the lives of Moses and Solomon. It was also thrilling to see how parallel their commissions were: Man building a temple in which God would dwell and manifest His life and glory to man!

I could hardly wait to see the third man with a parallel commission. It is not too difficult to see ahead and figure out who the third man might be. I had no idea how exciting it was going to be as the Lord began to reveal this third man to me from the Word.

THE THIRD COMMISSION

The Prophet Zechariah had a visitation of God and the Word of the Lord came to him saying,

> *"Behold, the Man whose name is the **Branch**! From His place He shall branch out, and He shall build the temple of the Lord; Yes, He shall build the temple of the Lord..."* **Zechariah 6:12,13**

Jeremiah the prophet also prophesied about this matter,

> *"Behold, the days are coming, says the Lord, That I will raise to David a Branch of righteousness; A King shall reign and prosper, and execute judgment and righteousness in the earth. In His days Judah will be saved, and Israel will dwell safely; Now this is His name by which He will be called: **The Lord our Righteousness!**"*
> **Jeremiah 23:5,6**

Jeremiah's prophecy leads us to the Lord our Righteousness whom we know in the new covenant is Jesus. Paul said,

> "But of Him you are in Christ Jesus, who became for us wisdom from God, and **righteousness** and sanctification and redemption..." ***I Corinthians 1:30***

Isaiah also spoke of **"...The Branch..."** in prophecy,

> "There shall come forth a Rod from the stem of Jesse, and a **Branch** shall grow out of his roots. The Spirit of the Lord shall rest upon Him, the Spirit of wisdom and understanding, the Spirit of counsel and might, the Spirit of knowledge and of the fear of the Lord." ***Isaiah 11:1***

"...Rod...", "...stem...", "...branch...", and "...roots..." are all terms used to describe descendants. Isaiah is foretelling the coming of the Branch as a descendant through Jesse.

Luke brings it into focus for us,

> "...I have found David the son of Jesse, a man after My own heart, who will do all My will. From this man's seed, according to the promise, God raised up for Israel a Savior, Jesus..." ***Acts 13:22,23***

We see clearly the man whose name is **"...The Branch..."**, the descendant of Jesse through David, is Jesus.

We can go back to Zechariah's prophesy and substitute our new information about **"...The Branch..."**

Temple of Glory

> *"Behold the man whose name is The Branch (Jesus), He shall grow up out of His place, and He shall build the temple of the Lord..."* **Zechariah 6:12,13**

By inspiration of God the Holy Ghost Zechariah prophesied, foretelling the work of Jesus. He said Jesus *("...The Branch...")* was going to build the temple of the Lord. If Jesus was to build the temple of the Lord, then that would be God's will for Him because everything Jesus did was God's will. Jesus said,

> *"...I came down from heaven, not to do My own will, but the will of Him Who sent Me..."* **John 6:38**

Zechariah's prophecy foretelling the work of Jesus reveals the will of God for Jesus. The will of God regarding the work He wants a man to do is just another way of saying God's commission for a man. So, then, Zechariah's prophecy gives us a description of the Father's commission for Jesus: **Build the Temple of the Lord.** Our third man with a parallel commission to that of Moses and Solomon is Jesus, Himself.

Moses and Solomon fulfilled their commissions. Both of their completed temples are spoken of in the Old Testament. How about Jesus, has He fulfilled His commission?

Chapter Three

THE COMMISSION OF JESUS

In order to answer the question, whether or not Jesus has fulfilled His commission to build the Temple of the Lord, we need to understand two things:

1. The time frame for the commission to be fulfilled.

2. What the Temple of the Lord is.

Zechariah's prophecy points us in the right direction to understand the first point. The Spirit of the Lord said through Zechariah,

> "Behold, the Man whose name is the BRANCH! From His place He shall branch out, and He shall build the Temple of the Lord." **Zechariah 6:12**

It was the man as *"...The Branch..."* commissioned to build the Temple. Since *"...The Branch..."* is Jesus, in order for the prophecy to be fulfilled, the building of the Temple could not be done until Jesus became a man. This brings us into the dispensation of the New Testament. Our search for description of the Temple of the Lord will be New Testament terms.

Moses and Solomon operated under the old covenant in an external relationship with God. This required the temples in their commissions to be built with natural materials. However, the Temple of the Lord in the New Testament is of a different nature.

Temple of Glory

THE TEMPLE OF THE LORD

The Temple in the New Testament can be seen on two levels: *the individual level* and *the corporate level*. Paul wrote of the Temple in letters he wrote to the Church at Corinth. He said,

> *"...do you not know that your body is the temple of the Holy Spirit who is it you, whom you have from God, and you are not your own?"* **I Corinthians 6:19**

He had already asked them,

> *"Do you not know that you are the temple of God and that the Spirit of God dwells in you?"*
> **I Corinthians 3:16**

God actually dwells in every person who is born again. Every believer is a temple of the Lord on the *individual level*.

In writing to Christians Peter said they were *"...living stones, were being built up a spiritual house..."* **I Peter 2:5**

Peter used the terminology *"...spiritual house..."* for what was to be built. Look what Paul wrote in his letter to the Church at Ephesus:

> *"Now, therefore, you are no longer strangers and foreigners, but fellow citizens with the saints and members of the household of God, having been built on the foundation of the apostles and prophets, Jesus Christ Himself being the chief cornerstone, in whom the whole building, being fitted together, grows into a holy temple in the Lord, in whom you also are being built together for a dwelling place of God in the spirit."*
> **Ephesians 2:19-22**

The Commission of Jesus

One Temple is the goal, to serve as a habitation or dwelling place for God.

This is parallel to the commissions for Moses and Solomon where the temple was to be built as a dwelling place for God to dwell among his people. The new covenant is established on better promises. The only thing better than God dwelling near you, as in the old covenant, is God dwelling in you! On the *corporate level*, then, every believer is a living stone to be fitly joined together with other living stones to become one Temple of the Lord as a habitation of God.

UNFULFILLED COMMISSION

By understanding what the Temple of the Lord is in the New Testament, we see Jesus' commission is unfulfilled. There are many persons yet to be born again who will become individual temples of the Lord. Corporately, all believers as living stones must be fit together to complete the main sanctuary. Because many are not yet born again, there is an inadequate supply of building materials to build the Temple. Therefore, the Temple of the Lord is incomplete: ***Jesus' commission is not yet finished!***

The period of time in which this unfinished Temple is to be built is New Testament dispensation. The Temple of the Lord is individual believers as temples fit together corporately becoming one Temple. One final understanding is needed to see who it is that has actually been commissioned to build the Temple.

Temple of Glory

It was God the Father who commissioned Moses and Solomon to build the temples in the Old Testament. And it was God the Father who commissioned *"...The Branch..."* to build the Temple in the New Testament. We have seen clearly from the Word *"...The Branch..."* is Jesus. But there is something we need to see about Jesus. While Jesus as the Word never changes, the same yesterday, today, and forever, the manifestation of Jesus as the Word does change.

He has not always been manifest to the world in the same form. Before Jesus was clothed in flesh, He was the invisible Word of God. He was still the Word after He was clothed in flesh but changed in manifestation to visible human form. After His resurrection from the dead, His state changed again into a glorified body. Paul explained these things to the Corinthians,

> *"So also is the resurrection of the dead. The body is sown in corruption, it is raised in incorruption. It is sown in dishonor, it is raised in glory. It is sown in weakness, it is raised in power. It is sown a natural body, it is raised a spiritual body. There is a natural body, and there is a spiritual body."* ***I Corinthians 15:42-44***

It was always the same Word but manifest in different forms: from invisible Word to visible flesh and blood to glorified flesh and bone. These were three different manifestations of the unchanging Word of God. There is one other manifestation we need to see necessary for our understanding regarding Jesus and His commission.

The Commission of Jesus

THE BODY OF CHRIST

Paul wrote,

> *"For as the body is one and has many members, but all the members of that one body, being many, are one body, so also is Christ. For by one Spirit we were all baptized into one body, whether Jews or Greeks, whether slaves or free, and have all been made to drink into one Spirit. For in fact the body is not one member but many. If the foot should say, "Because I am not a hand, I am not of the body," is it therefore not of the body? And if the ear should say, "Because I am not an eye, I am not of the body," is it therefore not of the body?" If the whole body were an eye, where would be the hearing? If the whole body were hearing, where would be the smelling? But now God has set the members, each one of them, in the body just as He pleased. And if they were all one member, where would the body be? But now indeed there are many members, yet one body. And the eye cannot say to the hand, "I have no need of you"; nor again the head to the feet, "I have no need of you." No, much rather, those members of the body which seem to be the weaker are necessary. And those members of the body which we think to be less honorable, on these we bestow greater honor; and our unpresentable parts have greater modesty, but our presentable parts have no need. But God composed the body, having given greater honor to that part which lacks it, that there should be no schism in the body, but that the members should have the same care for one another. And if one member suffers, all the members suffer with it; or if one member is honored, all the members rejoice with it. Now you are the body of Christ, and members individually."*
>
> ***I Corinthians 12:12-27***

You and I as Christians are members of the Body of Christ. It is easy to spiritualize away the mysterious meaning of this

Temple of Glory

truth. It is obvious we do not make up one physical body with hands, legs, and other recognizable natural body parts. As a result, we have considered ourselves only *"...spiritually..."* part of the Body of Christ. Paul wrote by inspiration of God the Holy Spirit,

> *"...we are members of His body, of His flesh, and of His bones..."* **Ephesians 5:30**

How can these things be? This is a question asked many times concerning things in the kingdom of God. Jesus told Nicodemus a man must be born again to see the kingdom of God. Nicodemus asked, *"How can these things be?"*. We ask how can we be one flesh and bone body with Jesus as the head? The Holy Spirit told us through the writing of Paul it is as,

> *"...a man leaves his father and mother, and shall be joined unto his wife, and they two shall be one flesh. This is a great mystery: but I speak concerning Christ and the Church."* **Ephesians 5:31,32**

Christ and the Church are one Body!

Although we are many individual members, God sees us as one flesh and bone body with Christ Jesus as the Head.

When the commission was given to the man whose name is *"...The Branch..."* whom we know to be Jesus, it was given to the whole man Jesus, Head, body, and all. The commission is as applicable to us, the body, as to Jesus, the Head. The *"...Great Commission..."* of the Church was not given to the Church by Jesus but was given to Jesus, body and all, by the Father: Build the Temple of the Lord! You and I are a manifestation of Jesus' body on the earth.

This certainly does not diminish the importance of evangelism *(...gathering building materials...)*. Without the proper number of stones, the Temple cannot be completed. ***Evangelism is a vital part of the great commission, but it must be seen in its proper place as only one part of many.***

Truly the fruit of evangelism, the new birth of a human spirit, is one of the most miraculous events on the face of the earth. The virgin birth was miraculous above that of any other birth. Without the birth of the holy child Jesus, all of us who are Gentiles would still be lost and alienated from God without hope in the world. Born again Jews would still be living under the old covenant looking at the promise of salvation as a future event. However, Jesus had to do more than just be born miraculously on the earth in order to bring salvation to Jew and Gentile alike. He had to grow out of infancy into manhood. He had to do all the works the Father assigned Him. He had to die on Calvary. He had to be resurrected. He had to place His blood on the altar for us all. ***Thank God for Jesus' miraculous birth!*** But aren't you glad there was more to Jesus' earthly life and ministry than just a miraculous birth?!

New birth for believers is important and vital, but there is more to our earthly lives and ministries than being born again. God desires, and we should desire, that every person in the world be born again. Even so, if every person in the world were born again today, the commission the Father gave Jesus to build the Temple of the Lord would not be fulfilled. ***There is more to the commission than just gathering living stones, no matter how important this part is!***

TEACHING

Teaching the believers to observe all things that Christ commanded is important and vital as part of the commission as well. Paul told us we were not to be conformed to this world but transformed by the renewing of our minds to know the will of God. Because God's Word is His will as the believers are taught the Word, the process of teaching helps them know God's will. John said by inspiration of the Holy Spirit that he prayed,

> *"...that you may prosper in all things and be in health, just as your soul prospers..."* ***III John 2***

God wants all believers to grow to a place of supernatural health and prosperity. Health and prosperity come as our souls prosper through the Word.

> *"All scripture is given by inspiration of God, and is profitable for doctrine, for reproof, for correction, for instruction in righteousness, that the man of God may be complete, thoroughly equipped for every good work."*
> ***II Timothy 3:16,17***

Teaching, too, is only part of the commission. God desires more than individually transformed believers. He has commissioned a temple to be built; a body functioning in the earth as one body! This means individually transformed believers must be united in order to function as one body in the earth. Yes, we were baptized into one body by one Spirit at our new birth, which means we are united spiritually. More than this, though, God expects us to achieve practical unity which is men walking together in agreement as doers of the Word. Just like James said, *"...faith without works is dead..."* ***James 2:26***, so, too, spiritual unity without men walking together in agreement as doers of the Word is barren. This type of unity is not achieved by teaching alone. Men must put works with their faith by walking together in faith.

Evangelism, teaching, and walking together as doers of the Word are all parts of the overall task of producing one body on the earth. In order to get a better understanding of how comprehensive the commission to build the Temple of the Lord is, compare it with a natural building. Building the Temple of the Lord is the most enormous building project ever undertaken. Therefore, our comparison between the spiritual building and a natural building must be enormous.

Imagine building a major shopping center with hundreds of stores all enclosed in an indoor mall. Consider all of the complex facets of the building process: foundation, plumbing, wiring, walls, windows, roof...so many parts to be done it takes hundreds of workers.

Which construction component is the most important? Our first assumption may be the foundation. But after careful thought, we realize all of the parts are important and vital to the completion of the building. With any one of the construction components missing, such as wiring or roofing, the building would be incomplete. If all the components have been done well except for plumbing, when the pipes begin to leak, the whole building suffers.

Building a natural building is a complex process involving many components of construction. The commission to build the Temple of the Lord is equally complex. Understanding this commission and seeing its many components is the first requirement necessary for us to achieve the success God intends us to have!

There are three requirements necessary for success:

1. Understanding the commission.

2. Supernatural personnel with divinely given abilities.

3. Adequate provision of material and funds.

Now that we have a general understanding of our commission, what about supernatural personnel?

SUPERNATURAL PERSONNEL

God commissioned the Church to build a spiritual building according to His pattern and specifications. This would be impossible for natural man with only natural abilities. Thank God, it is His responsibility to provide supernatural personnel and abilities to build the Temple.

Understanding the specific purpose for which these supernatural personnel are needed will make it easier to identify them. Both the individual level and the corporate level need constructing in the Temple building project. On the individual level the believer, as a temple of the Lord, is expected to mature in two areas: his knowledge of God in him and who he is in Christ. Jesus said life eternal is,

> *"...that they may know You, the only true God, and Jesus Christ whom You have sent..."* **John 17:3**

Life eternal spoken of in this verse is not quantity of days, but rather, quality of life as God has it. God's life, nature, and abilities were imparted into the believer the moment a person believed. God, Himself, came to dwell in the new believer. However, this new life in us does not cause us to be changed in all areas automatically. It is our intimate knowledge of the Father and the Son which causes this life to be manifest in and through us. The intimate knowledge is not knowledge about, but rather, relationship with the Father and the Son. The greater the depth of relationship you have with anyone, the more you know them.

The Word says the new believer is a babe in Christ. He does not know who he is in Christ. As he begins to grow by partaking of the sincere milk of the Word, he comes to a place of maturity just like a natural child grows to maturity. It is a mature believer who walks in the earth doing the very works

Temple of Glory

Jesus did. Natural babies do not come to a place of maturity all by themselves. They need parenting. So, too, spiritual babies need help to mature in the Lord.

Many times we have not given babes in Christ an opportunity to develop their relationship with God before we expect them to go out onto the front lines as highly trained soldiers to do battle with a merciless enemy. It is a well-equipped and well-trained soldier, skilled in the use of his weapons, who will be victorious in battle. Therefore, we need supernatural personnel to help babes in Christ come to a place of maturity in their knowledge of God in them and who they are in Christ. This maturity or perfection will cause the believers to be able to walk supernaturally successful on the earth.

On the corporate level the believers as living stones are expected to be built together in unity. Jesus prayed,

> "...that they all may be one, as You, Father, are in Me, and I in You; that they also may be one in Us, that the world may believe that You sent Me..." **John 17:21**

How is our unity together with God going to provide credibility to the world that Jesus was sent by the Father? Nicodemus' interaction with Jesus helps our understanding in this matter,

> "...Rabbi, we know that You are a teacher come from God; for no one can do these signs that You do unless God is with him..." **John 3:2**

The Commission of Jesus

Jesus elaborated on this matter of God united with Him during a discussion with His disciples when Philip asked Him to show them the Father. Jesus responded by telling Philip if he had seen Jesus, he had seen the Father. He went on to say,

> *"Believe Me that I am in the Father and the Father in Me, or else believe Me for the sake of the works themselves."* **John 14:11**

Jesus was explaining to Philip it was because of His intimate relationship of unity with the Father that He was able to walk in the supernatural. Then, He told Philip specifically to believe He was united with the Father or else believe for the work's sake. In other words, the supernatural works gave credibility to the fact God was united with Jesus. Not only did the supernatural works give credibility to Jesus' unity with the Father, but they were a direct result of this unity.

When Jesus prayed that we would be one just as He was united with the Father, He knew our unity with one another in God and God in us would produce supernatural works through us. These supernatural works among us would give testimony to the world that God sent the Christ to live among us. Such unity does not come automatically in the Church. We need supernatural personnel to help build us into one unified body on the earth.

We are looking for supernatural personnel, then, to help build the Temple on both individual and corporate levels. Their task is to perfect the saints and unite the body. The apostle Paul wrote on these very matters in his letter to the Ephesians. He said Christ gave gifts unto men. Then he identified these gifts,

> *"...He Himself gave some to be apostles, some prophets, some evangelists, and some pastors and teachers..."*
> **Ephesians 4:11**

Whenever I receive a gift, because I am a very practical person, I like to know what function the gift has. Do you remember some years ago a special gift item was marketed around Christmas time: a pet rock. Many people rushed out and bought pet rocks to give their friends. Thank God, Christ has not given us any pet rocks. His gifts are for a purpose, always functional.

Paul continued to explain the purpose of these gifts from Christ are,

> *"...For the equipping of the saints for the work of the ministry, for the edifying of the body of Christ, till we all come to the unity of the faith and of the knowledge of the Son of God, to a perfect man, to the measure of the stature of the fullness of Christ..."* **Ephesians 4:12,13**

There are other supernatural personnel God has provided for the building of the temple, but they will be discussed in Part Two. It is enough here to satisfy our second requirement for success to see apostles, prophets, evangelists, pastors, and teachers as the supernatural ministry gifts Christ has given to perfect the saints and unify the Body.

ADEQUATE PROVISION OF MATERIALS AND FUNDS

No matter how much we understand our commission or how many supernatural personnel we have, we still must have adequate provision of material and funds in order to be successful. For the temple to be built on the earth we need natural materials and money. You cannot go to the airline company and say, *"I am called and commissioned by God to go to Africa",* and expect the airline to invite you to fly free. No, they will say, *"That's fine, now give us this much money and you can go to Africa."*

The unchanging God, who required the Israelites to provide the materials and funds for the tabernacle to be built, still requires His people to fund His work in the earth. The Lord supernaturally meets our individual needs

> *"...according to His riches in glory by Christ Jesus..."*
> **Philippians 4:19**

In this same supernatural way, the Lord provided the wealth of Egypt for the Israelites as individuals when they were delivered from the Egyptians. That is His covenant relationship with us as Jehovah Jirah: the Lord our Provider. As we are supernaturally blessed as individuals, He expects us to give back to Him so His work can be done on the earth, as we saw in **Exodus 25:1-9** concerning the Israelites.

> *"...The Father of lights, with whom is no variation or shadow of turning..."* **James 1:17**

The unchanging God supplies our individual needs, but then requires us as individual members of the body of Christ to fund the building of the temple of the Lord on the earth.

The actual building materials of which the temple is made are *"...living stones...".* These materials are not made with human hands nor are they natural materials such as those

Temple of Glory

given for the building of the tabernacle in Moses' commission. However, there are many materials needed to help the work of the Lord be done on the earth such as natural buildings in which believers can meet, printed literature, planes, cars, TV stations, radio stations, and other such materials.

Paul's letter to the Corinthians gives us further insight in this matter,

> *"Who ever goes to war at his own expense? Who plants a vineyard and does not eat of its fruit? Or who tends a flock and does not drink of the milk of the flock? Do I say these things as a mere man? Or does the law say the same also? For it is written in the law of Moses, "You shall not muzzle an ox while it treads out the grain." Is it oxen God is concerned about? Or does He say it altogether for our sakes? For our sakes, no doubt, this is written, that he who plows should plow in hope, and he who threshes in hope should be partaker of his hope. If we have sown spiritual things for you, is it a great thing if we reap your material things? If others are partakers of this right over you, are we not even more? Nevertheless we have not used this right, but endure all things lest we hinder the gospel of Christ. Do you not know that those who minister the holy things eat of the things of the temple, and those who serve at the altar partake of the offerings of the altar? Even so the Lord has commanded that those who preach the gospel should live from the gospel."* **I Corinthians 9:7-14**

We know in the setting at Corinth Paul made tents to provide money for his own personal needs. We do not know in this specific case whether the Lord directed Paul to do this or if Paul did this out of his own will. One thing we do know about God's will, *"...the Lord ordained that they which preach the gospel should live of the gospel."* In the context of which this verse was written, Paul was saying that those receiving ministry are the ones to give.

The Commission of Jesus

When we see all three of these requirements for success met in the Body of Christ, in a local assembly, or in an individual's life, the measure of success in which we walk will be increased according to the level the requirements are met. For example: Suppose a church does not understand their responsibility or benefit in giving finances. It will be harder for this local church to do the work of the ministry than if the people were liberal, cheerful givers. The more the people give, the easier, in one sense, the work of the ministry will become. As the giving requirement is met more fully, success will rise proportionately. The same holds true for all three requirements. These requirements must be met for the Body of Christ to achieve God's expectations on the earth. Meeting these requirements will make us corporately and individually successful.

Temple of Glory

Chapter Four

SUPERNATURAL PERSONNEL

In Part One we saw God's plan for man: **God united with man so He and man become one.** We discovered the purpose of this plan is to bring man back to a place of sonship, through love, ruling over creation. In order for God's plan and purpose to be successful on the earth, God commissioned Jesus to build the Temple of the Lord. This temple is to be the basis for both the plan and purpose becoming operational on the earth. To make sure success is achieved God has given supernatural personnel through Christ to see the temple built. God supernaturally supplies our needs expecting in return that we freely give for His work to be done. Freely we have received, freely we are to give.

Part Two of this book is going to focus primarily on supernatural personnel. God has already given the gifts of apostle, prophet, evangelist, pastor, and teacher as supernatural personnel for the temple to be built. Yet we do not see these gifts functioning at a very high level on the earth today. If God above has given them as gifts to us, they must be good and perfect because James said,

> *"Every good gift and every perfect gift is from above, and comes down from the Father of lights, with whom there is no variation or shadow of turning..."*
> **James 1:17**

We have already seen Christ gave the gifts specific purposes. If they are good and perfect gifts given for specific purposes yet we do not see them in operation very much, there are two possible reasons why:

1. We do not need them any longer, or

2. We do not understand the gifts or our need for them.

We still need them because Paul wrote they have been given,

> *"...till we all come to the unity of the faith and of the knowledge of the Son of God, to a perfect man, to the measure of the stature of the fullness of Christ..."*
> **Ephesians 4:13**

We are not all walking in the unity of the faith so we can rule out reason number one as the why we do not see the gifts in operation very much. This leaves reason number two, which means we do not accurately understand the gifts and our need for them. We can begin our discussion from this point.

> *"And God has appointed these in the church: first apostles, second prophets, third teachers, after that miracles, then gifts of healings, helps, administrations, varieties of tongues..."* **I Corinthians 12:28**

Paul was writing here by inspiration of God the Holy Spirit concerning ministry gifts in the Church.

Supernatural Personnel

The Lord opened my eyes to see He had set the ministry gifts in the Church. He began showing me various reasons why they have been set in the Church. Going back to ***Ephesians chapter four*** consider a connection between verses ***11, 12, and 13.***

> *"And He Himself gave some to be apostles, some prophets, some evangelists, and some pastors and teachers, for the equipping of the saints, for the work of ministry, for the edifying of the body of Christ, till we all come to the unity of the faith and of the knowledge of the Son of God, to a perfect man, to the measure of the fullness of Christ..."* ***Ephesians 4:11-13***

God has given the apostle, the prophet, the evangelist, the pastor, and the teacher as five ministry gifts responsible for perfecting the saints and bringing the Body to a place of unity. Even though I had read these verses many times before, I had never seen this connection. All five of the offices have a part to play in perfecting the saints and bringing the Body to a place of unity!

Even the evangelist, whose ministry we have thought of as exclusively to the lost, is included in the list of ministry gifts responsible for perfecting the saints. There is something in the office of evangelist which the saints need in order to be perfected. The evangelist is primarily to minister to the lost, but we need this ministry as an evangelist to us as believers.

When I first saw these things, I was greatly blessed and somewhat overwhelmed. Why hadn't I seen this before? Why weren't these five gifts in greater manifestation ***in the***

Church? We are all interested in seeing the saints perfected and the Church unified. We should desire anything God gives to help in these tasks. Yet, here are gifts given by God expressly for these tasks not in operation much in the Church. When I saw how these gifts were intended to help us fulfill our commission, I began to teach on the five-fold ministry. I taught how God has set these five offices ***in the Church***. And how they are God's supernatural personnel given for us to be able to build the temple of the Lord. All five offices have been given responsibility for the perfecting of the saints and the unifying of the body.

In the course of these teachings two questions began to appear as *"...stumbling blocks..."*:

1. What does "...in the Church..." mean; are all five offices supposed to be resident in every local church?

2. Who is in charge of the local church?

As I began to study and meditate on these questions, I saw teaching on the five-fold ministry was not teaching on some new form of church government nor trying to get all five ministry gifts staff positions in every local church. I know we must speak directly to these two questions, but they are not the primary consideration.

The primary consideration is not one of control in the local church, but, rather, "How do we perfect the saints and build the Church?" What we must face is the fact that all five offices are needed to perfect the saints and unify the Body. We must move in any direction necessary to see greater manifestations of these five offices in the Church.

Supernatural Personnel

The primary consideration is not one of control in the local church, but rather, *"How do we perfect the saints and build the Church?"* All five offices are needed to perfect the saints and unify the Body. We must move in any direction necessary to see greater manifestations of these five offices in the Church.

Revelation regarding the five-fold ministry is emphatically not teachings on church government and who is in charge of the local church. Neither is the revelation requiring all five offices to be resident in every local assembly. But the revelation is absolutely requiring ministry input from all five offices to perfect the saints and unify the Body. Anywhere there are saints, there needs to be consistent regular input into their lives from the apostle, the prophet, the evangelist, the pastor, and the teacher. God has made it very clear that *He* has set all five offices in the Church and that *He* has given each office their responsibilities. The primary focus of these responsibilities is to help perfect the saints and unify the Body.

From the 1950's to the turn of the twentieth century the Church on the earth has come a long way in understanding in many areas from the Church alive on the earth during the dark ages. However, we must not be content with how far we have come from the past. The past is not our standard. Christ is our standard, and we must constantly press toward being conformed to His image and living in His ways.

We do not want to fall short of the measure of the stature of the fullness of Christ. With no critical or judgemental spirit involved, we see two main areas in which the Church on the earth falls short:

> ➤ *...doing the works of Jesus (See John 14:12), and*

> ➤ *...the unity of the brethren!*

These assessments are not intended to bring condemnation to us, but rather to help bring us to an accurate assessment of where the Church is on the earth so we may see where we are and learn how to move forward!

FAITH MUST TURN TO SIGHT

We do not want to *"...think more highly of ourselves than we ought..."*. If our *"...faith..."* confession does not produce the life for which we are believing eventually, then we must honestly evaluate the operation of our faith according to the standard of Christ. His intent for us to walk in faith was for it to produce the life for which He was willing to die for us to possess! If our faith is not producing the life He intended for us to have, then we need to determine why.

Perhaps an example will serve us here. A number of year ago I heard of a young man endeavoring to live a life of faith. The weather man was forecasting heavy snowfall in the city in which the young man lived. Everyone who lived in this city was very concerned about heavy snowfalls interrupting their daily lives. The young man told everyone he saw there was no need to concern themselves because he had spo-

-ken to the weather and commanded the snow not to fall. The next day heavy snows fell on the city. All those with whom the young man had declared his faith proclamation asked what went wrong. They asked him what about all the snow on the ground, to which the young man replied, *"What snow"*. This is certainly not the operation of faith the Lord had in mind. This is clearly a failure in application of the young man's faith.

Faith produces living results! James wrote,

> *"...Someone will say, "You have faith, and I have works." Show me your faith without your works, and I will show you my faith by my works..."* **James 2:18**

Paul wrote to the Corinthians that *"...we walk by faith, not by sight..." (see* **II Corinthians 5:7)**. However, our faith must produce visible results in order for it to be a living faith. If we are in faith for our physical healing, a living faith will produce physical healing. If we are in faith for finances, a living faith will produce finances we can use to pay our bills. We are expected to walk by faith, but a living faith is expected to produce living results we can see.

WALK LIKE JESUS WALKED

We are all to have these same two goals, to walk like Jesus walked and to fulfill the expectations of the Lord. Jesus is very clear when He says:

"Most assuredly, I say to you, he who believes in Me, the works that I do he will do also; and greater works than these he will do, because I go to My Father."
John 14:12

"I do not pray for these alone, but also for those who will believe in Me through their word: that they all may be one, as You, Father, are in Me, and I in You; that they also may be one in Us, that the world may believe that You sent Me." **John 17:20,21**

However, the contemporary Church is not meeting these goals. This statement is not meant to condemn, but rather to cause us to evaluate our condition by faith, and find out what we must do to move in a different direction than the one on which we have been. It is the Lord's will for everyone who believes to do the works He did and to be one with Him and the Father. The world needs to know that the Father sent Jesus, and is sending us, to give them the good news that they, too, can be saved, healed, delivered, and transformed into the very image of Christ. We must determine how to move this direction!

We have already seen it takes supernatural personnel with divinely given abilities to meet our goal. What exactly does it mean for all five ministry gifts to be involved in perfecting the saints and bringing the Church into unity? Perhaps we can begin with a focus on *"...perfecting the saints..."*

ALL FIVE MINISTRY GIFTS NEEDED

The term *"...perfecting..."* does not mean the state of perfection, but rather to make *"...mature..."* The maturity for which we are looking is spiritual maturity. Paul wrote,

Supernatural Personnel

> *"...till we come to the unity of the faith and of the knowledge of the Son of God, to a perfect man, to the measure of the stature of the fullness of Christ..."* **Ephesians 4:13**

It is *"...knowing..."* God which produces life eternal or God's kind of life in us. When we have God's kind of life at work in us like Jesus had working in Him during His earthly ministry, then we will do the same works He did. He told the disciples it was God in Him doing the works He did. God's will for the saints to reach this kind of maturity or *"...perfection..."* is for all five offices of ministry to be in manifestation on the behalf of the saints. However, ministry to the saints to help them mature is only part of the responsibilities of the ministry gifts.

Consider the office of prophet working through the man Agabus as recorded in ***Acts 11:27-30***. He foretold a future dearth coming throughout all the world. While this prophetic manifestation did not directly help perfect the saints, it brought great blessing to the brethren in Judaea because the disciples at Antioch sent financial assistance to them as a result of the Word of the Lord spoken through the office of prophet. Perfecting the saints is only part of the responsibilities God assigned to the five offices of ministry.

Another example of diverse responsibilities of one of the offices of ministry can be seen in Philip, the evangelist. Philip, as an evangelist, went down to the city of Samaria and preached Christ to unbelievers. There were many miracles and many people came to the Lord. This was a tremendous manifestation of the office of evangelist.

Philip was concerned about telling the lost of Samaria the good news that Jesus had died to save them. He was not ministering directly to the saints to help Christians grow in their knowledge of the Son of God. Philip was in Samaria ministering to the lost and not to the saints.

Typically, even if the contemporary church accepts the truth that the five offices of ministry are still viable for today, our understanding has been restricted to the functions of the offices not related to actually imparting *"...knowledge..."* of our God by which the saints are to grow to maturity: Apostles start churches, prophets prophesy, evangelists win the lost, etc. While there are elements of truth to these functions, this view fundamentally eliminates the primary functions for which the offices have been given: *"...perfect..."* the saints and help bring them to a place of unity. Surely not the only causes for the restriction in our understanding, but perhaps a start to help eliminate the restrictions:

1. Past abuse of the gifts.

2. Lack of teaching on the gifts.

3. Very little demonstration of the gifts.

PAST ABUSE OF THE GIFTS

Men and women have used impersonation as a means to perpetuate some corrupt motive throughout history. This is true in relation to the five offices of ministry. A person cannot be an apostle, prophet, evangelist, pastor, or teacher unless

God wills it. Just because men have abused the gifts of God does not make the gifts corrupted. The abuse merely reveals the corruption in men's hearts. Yet we have typically rejected the gifts of God because of such abuses, rather than seeing the corruption of men.

If a man impersonates an officer in the army, we do not think badly of army officers or fear all army officers are imposters. If a man pretends to be a bank president in order to rob the bank, we do not think badly of bank presidents or fear all bank presidents are bank robbers. In both cases we see the corruption in the heart of the persons trying to be something they are not to achieve some corrupt end.

Men have been doing evil things in the name of Christianity for many years. One man, in the name of a gift of ministry, took hundreds of people from the U.S.A. to a foreign country and led them into suicide in the name of Christianity. Evil men have abused the offices of ministry throughout the history of the Church, but we cannot throw away the necessary gifts God gave us simply because of corrupt motives of evil men. Anytime a doctrine or gift in the kingdom of God is abused, a fear develops about that doctrine or gift. The principle of fear is a subtle thing, not like the fear of a poisonous snake.

PRINCIPLE OF FEAR

Even in the churches who believe in the manifestations of the Spirit, the actual number of manifestations in any given corporate gathering seem to be extremely limited in number.

Temple of Glory

Very often the reason there are not more manifestations of the Spirit is because a *"...fear..."* has developed among the people.

The fear is usually a result of someone in the congregation having given an inaccurate prophetic utterance or one of the other manifestations of the Spirit. They may have even led a believer astray with the inaccuracy of their utterance. Under these types of conditions an attitude begins to develop: *"We believe in the manifestations of the Spirit of God, but, bless God, you better not make a mistake if you are the vessel through whom the Spirit brings the manifestation."* Who would yield, even if it was to the gentle Holy Spirit, under these conditions? We are to desire accuracy in the manifestations of the Spirit. However, if a believer is inaccurate, there is a holy means of judging the inaccuracy without producing harm to the person who was inaccurate. God has not given us the spirit of fear.

This same type of *"...fear..."* is partially responsible for keeping us from accepting all five of the offices of ministry. We generally accept an evangelist as an evangelist; or a pastor as a pastor; or a teacher as a teacher. If we are in a corporate meeting of the church and a minister is introduced as an evangelist, we can accept that; or as a pastor; or as a teacher. Even if we ask these ministers to which office they are called, and they respond evangelist, pastor, or teacher, we can still accept that. However, if some minister is introduced as an apostle or prophet, typically fear signals go up. If we ask a minister about the office to which he believes he is called, and he responds apostle or prophet we balk. It is not only because of past abuses that we fear to accept these offices of ministry. It is also because of a lack of accurate teaching on the offices of ministry.

LACK OF TEACHING ON THE GIFTS

John wrote that Jesus,

> *"...came to His own, and His own did not receive Him. But as many as received Him, to them He gave the right to become children of God, to those who believe in His name..."* **John 1:11,12**

How did people come to a place to be able to receive or accept Jesus as their Savior? Paul told us,

> *"For whosoever calls on the name of the Lord shall be saved. How then shall they call on Him in whom they have not believed? And how shall they believe in Him of whom they have not heard? And how shall they hear without a preacher? And how shall they preach unless they are sent? ...So then faith comes by hearing, and hearing by the word of God."* **Romans 10:13,14,17**

In other words, the only way a person can accept Jesus as Lord and Savior is to be taught about Him. This same principle holds true for everything of God. If you want people to accept the ministry of the Holy Spirit, you must teach on the Holy Spirit. If you want people to accept healing as part of the atonement, you must teach on healing. If we want people to accept all five offices of ministry, we must teach on all five offices of ministry.

If our teaching is going to produce life in others, it must first be alive in us. If we are going to teach healing to others, we must be walking in God's supernatural healing ourselves. Otherwise, we are ministering the letter of the Word and not the spirit and life. Ministry of the letter promotes the doctrine of man. If we are going to teach others to accept ministry gifts, then we must first accept them ourselves.

We must begin by accepting the five offices of ministry as gifts given to us by Jesus the Lord Himself. Secondly we must understand all five offices of ministry have been given *"...till we all come to the unity of the faith and of the knowledge of the Son of God, to a perfect man, to the measure of the stature of the fullness of Christ..."* In other words, all five of these offices are very much viable for today. We must accept apostles and prophets just as we accept pastors, teachers, and evangelists. All of these offices of ministry are holy and can only be held as a direct result of God's will.

Chapter Five

THE CALLING OF GOD

Generally, we have more easily accepted the offices of pastor, teacher, and evangelist over the offices of apostle and prophet because we have not understood what makes a person an apostle, prophet, evangelist, pastor, or teacher. Typically, what a person does has defined which office of ministry they hold. However, what you do does not determine who you are in the ministry. A person may win hundreds of people to the Lord and still not be an evangelist. Such a person may just be a very active individual Christian who understands the ministry of reconciliation. Whether or not a person is an evangelist is not determined by how many people they win to the Lord, but rather by the *"...calling..."* of God. God's calling in a person's life is what makes them an evangelist. The five offices of ministry are not entered into by our works of winning the lost, starting churches, or any other work we may do. The only way a person is an apostle, prophet, evangelist, pastor, or teacher is by the *"...calling..."* of Almighty God!

The Word of the Lord came to Jeremiah saying,

> *"Before I formed you in the womb I knew you; before you were born I sanctified you; I ordained you a prophet to the nations."* **Jeremiah 1:5**

We know Jeremiah was a prophet. But what made him a prophet? Scripture teaches it was the Word of the Lord which came to Jeremiah *"...sanctifying and ordaining him a prophet to the nations..."* even before he came out of the womb. When Jeremiah was lying in his mother's arms, just a newborn babe, he was a prophet! Even though he had not walked in the office, he was God-ordained and sanctified a prophet because it was God's will and calling which made him a prophet and not what he did in the ministry.

Certainly, what he did in ministry was according to his calling, but it was not what he did that determined his calling. God determined his calling and then Jeremiah ministered according to that calling. The authority and equipment for Jeremiah to minister supernaturally was available to him because of the call of God. It was not just the need for a prophet and Jeremiah's availability to God to meet the need that allowed him to minister in the office of prophet. No one can stand in God's supernaturally called offices and operate the authority and equipment of the office unless they are called to that office. We have already seen a man winning souls is not standing in the office of evangelist just because he wins souls. He may be doing the works of an evangelist, but he is not an evangelist. Only God's calling to the office of evangelist makes a person an evangelist.

If you happened upon an accident and administered first-aid to a person by setting his broken leg, that would not make you a doctor. You may even have a medical kit and have given the person an injection of pain killer. That still would not make you a doctor just because you did two things a doctor does.

The Calling of God

What made Jesus the Christ was not His death on the cross or His working of miracles. He was the Christ even in Mary's womb because that is who God called Him to be! Jesus' whole life revolved around God's will and calling for His life, which was determined by God even before the world began.

IDENTIFYING THE OFFICE

We have tried to determine who a person is in ministry by looking at what he does. We have given a very limited job description for each office and tried to fit everyone into one of these descriptions. For example: The apostle starts churches; The prophet prophesies; The evangelist wins the lost; The pastor is the shepherd of the local assembly; The teacher teaches the Word. Therefore, if a person starts churches, he must be an apostle. If a person prophesies, he must be a prophet.

We cannot accurately identify who a person is in ministry by just looking at what he does. Philip went down to the city of Samaria and won many people to the Lord. These people who were born again came together as believers for worship and instruction. They represented the beginning of a local assembly. Incorporating, getting a building, and putting a sign out front that reads, "First Church of Samaria" is not starting a church. People born into the kingdom are the Church. Philip, in getting people born again, started this church in the city of Samaria.

If we look at our job descriptions to identify who he is in ministry, we will see that our job-description list says apostles start churches. Therefore, since Philip started this church, he must be an apostle. However, Luke called Philip an *"...evangelist..."* in **Acts, 21:8**. Neither was Philip standing in the office of apostle to start this church, even though he knew he was an evangelist. Luke tells us,

> *"...Philip went down to the city of Samaria and preached Christ unto them. ...when they believed Philip as he preached the things concerning the kingdom of God and the name of Jesus Christ, both men and women were baptized..."* **Acts 8:5,12**

Philip was preaching Christ to the *"...lost..."* for them to receive Jesus as their Lord so they could be saved. He was not functioning as an apostle in any capacity. In fact, when the apostles at Jerusalem heard the City of Samaria had received Jesus, they sent the apostles Peter and John down to pray for the believers to receive the Holy Spirit and testify of Jesus and preach the Word of the Lord to the new local church.

We must not try to identify who a person is in ministry simply by seeing what the person is doing. If we use our limited job descriptions, we will make mistakes in accurately identifying who a person is in ministry, as in the case with Philip the evangelist.

RECOGNIZING YOUR CALLING

How does the minister recognize the office to which he has been called if it is not by what he does? And, is it even important for him to know the office to which he has been called?

The Calling of God

My wife and I acknowledged the call to the ministry in Bethel Temple in Arlington, Texas listening to Howard Foltz, Missionary Director of Eurasia Teen Challenge. At that time the Lord said He had called us to the ministry as missionaries and we were to serve Him full-time. Some months later we went to Bible school to prepare ourselves. Then, we joined a missionary organization, received their training, and departed for a foreign field as missionary Bible translators.

After a year or so on the field, I began to cry out to the Lord. I knew we were where the Lord had sent us, but I also knew this was not our final ministry. I knew in my heart this was just another phase of our training. I lost focus on what we were doing and began to seek God for my true identity. I longed for our final ministry. I wanted to know who I was in the ministry. All of my attention seemed to be focused on this quest.

I knew Bible translators and missionaries were full-time ministers of the Lord Jesus, but I also knew they were not listed as five-fold ministry gifts in the New Testament. I believed I was called to a five-fold ministry position, and I wanted to know who I was.

Then, the Lord spoke to me and told me I had rendered myself ineffective in what He had asked me to do today. He told me to be satisfied with the knowledge that I was called to the full-time ministry and was where He had sent me. He said He was putting me on a *one-day-at-a-time ministry relationship with Him*. He said I was to do what my hands found to

Temple of Glory

do when I got up in the morning, and He would direct me day by day. He said He would show me when it was time to change, and He would open my eyes to see who I was when the time was right.

For over two years I was content with this arrangement, living in the foreign field in a grass house in a mangrove swamp one day at a time. Then the Lord led us to move back to the U.S.A. for a change of direction in ministry. We relocated to Tulsa, Oklahoma still on the one-day-at-a-time program. I was happy to operate this way and had even forgotten about my desire to know who I was in the five-fold ministry.

One day, while driving down the road worshipping God, the Lord began to minister to me. He asked me, "Do you think a bird knows he is a bird?" I thought it was a very strange question, but I knew it was the Lord who was asking. I said, "No, Lord, I do not think a bird knows he is a bird." The Lord said, "Well, when the bird is first hatched, he lies in the nest without feathers, does not know how to fly, dig for worms, or make a nest. He does not know how to do any of the things a bird does except eat and sleep, and, yet, he is still a bird. Then one day after the mother bird teaches him all the things he must know as a bird, he graduates from the nest to go off on his own. Do you think on his graduation day he comes into some kind of awareness that he is a bird?" I said, "No, Lord, he just is what you have made him."

What He told me He confirmed through the Word. He took me to the writings of the Old Testament prophet Isaiah,

The Calling of God

> *"Listen, O coastlands, to Me, and take heed, you peoples from afar! The Lord has called Me from the womb; from the matrix of my mother He has made mention of my name. And He has made my mouth like a sharp sword; in the shadow of His hand He has hidden me, and made me a polished shaft; in His quiver He has hidden me. And He said to me, you are My servant, O Israel, in whom I will be glorified. Then I said, 'I have labored in vain. I have spent my strength for nothing and in vain; yet surely my just reward is with the Lord, and my work with my God. And now the Lord says, Who formed me from the womb to be His servant, to bring Jacob back to Him, so that Israel is gathered to Him (For I shall be glorious in the eyes of the Lord, and my God shall be my strength...)...* **Isaiah 49:1-5**

This was important information that Isaiah had been called and formed to be the servant of the Lord even before he was born.

Then the Lord took me to Jeremiah which added a little more information.

> *"...Then the word of the Lord came to me, saying: "Before I formed you in the womb I knew you; before you were born I sanctified you; I ordained you a prophet to the nations."* **Jeremiah 1:4,5**

These two Old Testament scriptures helped, but the Lord said He called me before the foundation of the world. I wanted clearer confirmation. The Lord showed me Jesus as an illustration.

> *"...knowing that you were not redeemed with corruptible things, like silver or gold, from your aimless conduct received by tradition from your fathers, but with*

> *the precious blood of Christ, as of a lamb without blemish and without spot. He indeed was foreordained before the foundation of the world, but was manifest in these last times for you..."* **I Peter 1:18-20**

Jesus' life and ministry was foreordained before the foundation of the world. That means everything the man Jesus is and was is a result of God's calling before the foundation of the world.

Maybe I asked too much, but I said, "Lord, I do not want to be presumptuous, but that was Jesus. How about us today?" Then, He led me to Paul's letter to Timothy.

> *"...(God) who has saved us and called us with a holy calling, not according to our works, but according to His own purpose and grace which was given to us in Christ Jesus before time began..."* **II Timothy 1:9**

Paul as Saul of Tarsus persecuted the Church as a Jewish zealot. Then, on the road to Damascus, he encountered the Lord Jesus whom he had been persecuting. His life was changed and he became a Christian and a minster. We know he was called to be an apostle because he opened nine of the epistles he wrote by introducing himself as an apostle.

> *"Paul, a servant of Jesus Christ, called to be an apostle, separated unto the gospel of God..."* **Romans 1:1**

In Paul's letter to the church at Galatia he added information about himself and his calling that will be very helpful to us in this matter.

The Calling of God

> *"...But when it pleased God, who separated me from my mother's womb and called me through His grace, to reveal His Son in me, that I might preach Him among the Gentiles..."* **Galatians 1:15,16**

Paul was separated or set apart unto the gospel from his mother's womb. Yet Paul was not always a Christian. He did not respond to the call to become a Christian until he encountered Jesus on the road to Damascus. We also know he was called to be an apostle, but he did not always function in that office. In the thirteenth chapter of Acts he is identified as a prophet and/or teacher, not an apostle. He is not known as an apostle until in the fourteenth chapter of Acts, many years after he had been in ministry.

He was called before the foundation of the world but did not walk in the calling all at once. He first acknowledged and accepted the calling to be a Christian, then to be a prophet and/or a teacher. God had not opened his eyes to see he was also called to be an apostle until God determined it was time. Then the Holy Spirit said,

> *"...Now separate to me Barnabas and Saul for the work to which I have called them..."* **Acts 13:2**

It was then that Paul acknowledged and accepted his calling to be an apostle.

God called me to a five-fold ministry position before the foundation of the world. I did not see it at first. I acknowledged and accepted my call to be a Christian, then to the full-time ministry. It took seven years in one phase of ministry before God determined it was time to open my eyes to see the office to which I had been called, so that I could move into the new phase of ministry.

We need to be sensitive to God to acknowledge and accept His callings within our lives. It is not a grievous thing where we seek and search for the office. It is an act of rest waiting openly on the Lord to show us who He has called us to be!

AUTHORITY & EQUIPMENT OF THE OFFICE

The Lord said when we acknowledged and accepted His call on our lives and went to Bible school to prepare ourselves for the ministry, we were just like the bird. The bird had to learn the ways of a bird even though he did not know who he was. That was true for our lives. When we went to Bible school we knew we were called, but we had no idea to which office we had been called. We only knew we were called to full-time ministry as missionaries. However, missionary is not listed as a five-fold ministry gift. At Bible school we only learned the ways of the ministry in general. There is a certain amount of general training for the ministry which could be given to anyone called to the ministry without knowing the office to which they have been called.

The Lord said there comes a time when everyone called to the ministry must know the office to which they have been called. He said He had placed authority and equipment in each office necessary for the person standing in each office to fulfill the responsibilities of the office to which the person had been called. If a person did not know the office to which he had been called, it would be difficult for him to effectively operate the authority and equipment of the office in order to fulfill the responsibilities of the office. Then, He gave me a natural world illustration.

The office of President of the United States of America: The charisma and personal skill of the man holding the office of President does not make the office powerful. The congress of the U.S.A. has vested authority and power into the office itself. Even in times when the office has been temporarily vacated because of Presidential assassination, the world still sees the office as present in our government and powerful.

There have been many men stand in the office of President. History has recorded some of them as good Presidents and some of them as bad ones. The office of the Presidency did not change: It has the same authority and power for a good or bad President. The difference was how well the man holding the office understood the office and how well he learned to use the authority and equipment of the office.

The Lord said He determined the time each person called to the ministry must know the office to which he had been called in order for that person to learn how to effectively use the authority and equipment of the office. The Lord said we had not tapped into a very large percentage of the authority and equipment of each office because we had exclusively used men to serve as examples of the offices. He said if we would look to Him, He would begin to expand our understanding of the authority and equipment in each office.

Temple of Glory

He said there was enough authority and equipment in His gifts of ministry to produce perfected saints and a unified body!

GOD'S RESPONSIBILITY

The Lord gave many other analogies comparing the U.S.A. political system and the ministry gifts. He talked about the election process. He said no matter how badly a person desires to become President, he cannot unless he is elected by the people. The candidate may be the wealthiest man in the world or the most educated or even the most qualified for the Presidency. However, if the people do not choose him, he cannot be President. It is the same with each of the five office. No person, regardless of his or her natural abilities, treasures, or talents, can become an apostle, prophet, evangelist, pastor, or teacher unless that person is called by God. No matter how many good things a person may do or how faithful they are or how badly they want to stand in one of these five offices of ministry, they cannot without the call.

He also said the calling is to a specific office or offices. As in the political system a person is elected, not to be a politician, but rather to a specific office. We do not elect five men to be politicians, and then they try to decide which one is President, Vice-President, Governor, Mayor, or City Councilman. There would be utter chaos and confusion with this type of election process and political system. Rather, we elect a particular person to a specific office.

The Calling of God

When the particular person is elected to a political office, they have a general idea of the authority and responsibilities of the political office to which they have been elected. However, even after a person is elected with a general understanding of the office to which he has been elected, it takes time of exercising the authority and executing the responsibilities of the office before he becomes proficient in the office. So, too, a person needs to know the office of ministry to which he has been called so he can learn what authority, equipment, and responsibilities are assigned to him in that office.

God, who calls us, is responsible for communicating His calling to us. We receive the call by faith just like all other things of God. The calling always remains an operation of faith on our part. No matter how successful we may become in the ministry, we still must exercise our faith to walk in the calling of God. So, too, God who calls us to the ministry, calls us to specific offices. He is responsible for opening our eyes to see the office to which He has called us. If we do not believe it is important to know the office, then we are not as open to receive specific information regarding the office to which God has called us.

We are not to become anxious in trying to discover the office to which we have been called. In the example from my own life living in the foreign field, I became so pre-occupied with trying to find the office that I became ineffective in what God had asked me to do right then. What I did was wrong as one extreme. But we do not want to be extreme in the opposite direction and be closed to knowing the office when it is time for us to know it.

Temple of Glory

These two positions are opposite ends of a continuum, and are both wrong. God expects us to...

1. Be open to His calling.

2. Understand the importance of knowing the office to which He has called us in order to learn the authority, equipment, and responsibilities of the office.

3. Rest in faith that He who has called us will open our eyes to see the office to which He has called us at His own time.

I walked almost seven years in one phase of full-time ministry without knowing the office to which I had been called. Basically, this phase of ministry was training for what was to come. It was not time for me to know the office. I was in the full-time ministry, walking in the plan of God for my life. There was an appointed time ordained by the Lord for Him to open my eyes to the specific office to which He had called me so He could move me into a new phase. He revealed the office to me in order to teach me what responsibilities went with the office and what authority and equipment He had placed within the office to help me fulfill my responsibilities. For a minister to be effective in ministry he must understand:

1. The responsibilities of the office to which he has been called.

2. The authority and equipment that accompanies the office so he may fulfill the responsibilities he has been given.

Chapter Six

RECEIVING A MINISTRY GIFT

Is it important that the Church identify who a minister is? Yes! It is very important that we accurately identify who a minister is. Jesus explained why as He talked to His twelve disciples.

> *"He who receives you receives Me, and he who receives Me receives Him who sent Me. He who receives a prophet in the name of a prophet shall receive a prophet's reward. And he who receives a righteous man in the name of a righteous man shall receive a righteous man's reward. And whoever gives one of these little ones only a cup of cold water in the name of a disciple, assuredly, I say to you, he shall by no means lose his reward."*
> **Matthew 10:40-42**

At the beginning of verse forty-one Jesus said,

> *"...He who receives a prophet in the name of a prophet shall receive a prophet's reward..."*

I never really understood this verse. What is the name of a prophet, Elijah or Isaiah? What is a prophet's reward? Then, the Holy Spirit gave me understanding. Jesus is saying in order for a person to receive a prophet's reward, he must first receive a prophet as a prophet. A prophet's reward is supernatural ministry from the office of prophet.

Temple of Glory

Elijah and the widow of Zarephath provide the perfect scriptural illustration. Without recounting the entire story we can begin with Elijah's prophecy to the widow,

> *"For thus says the Lord God of Israel: The bin of flour shall not be used up, nor shall the jar of oil run dry, until the day the Lord sends rain on the earth."*
> *I Kings 17:14*

We know the woman went and did according to the saying of Elijah and a miracle took place just as Elijah had prophesied.

The widow was not simply faced with a choice of obeying or disobeying the Word prophesied by Elijah. The Word would only have been a Word from the Lord if it had actually come through the prophet sent from the Lord. Any man could have said, *"...Thus saith the Lord..."*, but that would not have meant what the man said was the Word from the Lord. The first choice the widow faced was whether or not she accepted Elijah as a prophet of God. That is what Jesus meant when he said, *"...he who receives a prophet in the name of a prophet..."*. The widow had to receive Elijah, the prophet, as a prophet before she could receive the Word spoken through Elijah as a true Word from the Lord. When she received Elijah as a prophet, it was easier for her to receive the Word spoken by Elijah. Because she received Elijah as a prophet and went and did according to the Word prophesied through Elijah, she opened the door to be able to receive the prophet's reward. The prophet's reward was fulfillment of the Word spoken through the prophet. In other words, the prophet's reward was the supernatural ministry of a prophet.

Of course the miracle was a manifestation of the power of God. But the miracle began through the ministry of the prophet as he spoke *"...the Word of the Lord..."*. We are not taking any glory away from God. We are simply discovering how the spiritual principle, spoken by Jesus, works in people's lives. When we receive the prophet as a prophet, then we receive the prophet's reward.

ACCEPTANCE PRINCIPLE IN THE NEW TESTAMENT

Now, how does this principle apply to New Testament Christianity for apostles, prophets, evangelists, pastors, and teachers? The same way! Jesus went to Nazareth to minister to the people of His own home town. They only saw Him as Joseph's son, not as a man sent from God. The result was the principle in reverse: Their rejection closed the door on the supernatural. If you do not receive a prophet as a prophet, then you will not receive the prophet's reward. Jesus could not minister supernaturally in Nazareth and He explained why,

> *"... Assuredly, I say to you, no prophet is accepted in his own country..."* **Luke 4:24**

Truly the people were filled with unbelief just as the scripture says,

> *"...Now He did not do many mighty works there because of their unbelief..."* **Matthew 13:58**

However, it was not just a case of the people's doubt in God. It was also rejection of Jesus as a minister sent from God. John wrote about this acceptance/rejection principle regarding Jesus' ministry,

> "...*He (Jesus) came to His own, and His own did not receive Him. But as many as received Him, to them He gave the right to become children of God, to those who believe in His name...*" **John 1:11,12**

We can make a clear statement about this principle which will help us understand it better.

"Acceptance opens the door for the supernatural, rejection closes the door"!

It is extremely important to note that the acceptance or rejection is not toward God, but toward the disciples. Jesus said to the twelve disciples,

> "*He who receives you receives Me, and he who receives Me receives Him who sent Me.*" **Matthew 10:40**

The importance of identifying and accepting the minister is becoming clearer. According to Jesus' own words, if we accept the minister or disciple sent by God, then we have also accepted the Son and the Father. This opens the door for supernatural ministry to flow through the minister to us! If we can understand how this principle works, we can open the door to a level of supernatural ministry in which we have not yet walked.

Receiving a Ministry Gift

Whether we see the minister after the flesh or after the spirit is going to be the determining factor how we end up receiving them. The early church was confronted with this very same challenge. Whenever a minister's accomplishments are viewed as status symbols and become the basis for believers accepting them, corruption has already taken over. The church at Corinth had experienced this same temptation and fell under its power. The members of the church at Corinth were boasting,

> "...For when one says, "I am of Paul," and another, "I am of Apollos," are you not carnal? Who then is Paul, and who is Apollos, but ministers through whom you believed, as the Lord gave to each one? I planted, Apollos watered, but God gave the increase. So then neither he who plants is anything, nor he who waters, but God who gives the increase. ...Therefore let no one boast in men. For all things are yours: whether Paul or Apollos or Cephas, or the world or life or death, or things present or things to come, all are yours. And you are Christ's, and Christ is God's."
>
> **I Corinthians 3:4-7, 21-23**

Paul was not violating the Word when he said the planter and waterer were nothing. He knew both planter and waterer as individual Christians were the very righteousness of God in Christ Jesus. He was explaining to the Corinthians that after the flesh the ministers were nothing. When we look at the achievements done through the minister as if they were done in the power of the minister, we have seen the minister after the flesh. It is God who gives the increase!

Paul told us how to see one another,

> "*Therefore, from now on, we regard no one according to the flesh. Even though we have known Christ according to the flesh, yet now we know Him thus no longer. Therefore, if anyone is in Christ, he is a new creation; old things have passed away; behold, all things have become new.*" **II Corinthians 5:16,17**

Now we can apply our acceptance principle to ministers to open a new dimension of the spirit to us. There are three foundational components upon which our understanding will be based:

1. God calls men and women to stand in His ministry gift offices.

2. The offices of ministry are good and perfect gifts endowed by God with supernatural authority and equipment given by God to perfect the saints and unify the body.

3. A person who receives a prophet as a prophet will receive a prophet's reward.

We must not judge ministers after the flesh; to do so would be an act of carnality. These fleshly judgments can place a minister at either end of the same continuum, a celebrity minister or only a recent Bible school graduate. If we look at the newly graduated from Bible school minister as only knowing what he learned at Bible school, we close the door on the supernatural authority and equipment of his calling, if in fact he is truly called by God.

Receiving a Ministry Gift

Jesus told His disciples,

> *"He who receives you receives Me, and he who receives Me receives Him who sent Me."* **Matthew 10:40**

If our recently graduated from Bible school minister is called of God and we receive him as such, then according to Jesus we are receiving both the Father and the Son, too. When we receive the Father and the Son, we receive supernatural life in abundance. These faith actions cause us to bypass merely the experiences of the recently graduated Bible school minister and move instead to God's experiences and abilities.

There is a refinement we can make on this principle. If we know the office to which a person has been called and receive the person standing in that office, we set a spiritual law in motion. Jesus said,

> *"He who receives a prophet in the name of a prophet shall receive a prophet's reward..."* **Matthew 10:41**

We have already discovered the prophet's reward is the supernatural ministry of the office of the prophet. The office of prophet is a good and perfect gift endowed with God's supernatural authority and equipment to fulfill the specific responsibilities God has given the office and the particular minister standing in that office. Receiving the prophet's reward would be to receive God's supernatural authority and equipment from a good and perfect gift.

This takes ministry out of the realm of natural limitation according to the minister's experience and knowledge and moves it into a realm of unlimited ministry potential in God.

The minister actually being called by God is a pre-requisite for the principle to operate properly. Experience in ministry will help the minister flow more fluidly in the things of God. However, it is not just a minister's experience or desire to minister which makes supernatural ministry operate. There are principles by which supernatural ministry operates. We are simply endeavoring to learn how these principles work so we can open new doors of ministry to the Church.

If we could receive any office of ministry as a good and perfect gift from God, and if we could receive a particular believer as a believer called to stand in any particular office *(not according to the believer's past achievements, but according to God's endowments)*, we would unlock a flood gate for rivers of living water to flow to us! This principle will work for all five offices of apostle, prophet, evangelist, pastor, or teacher.

ACCEPTANCE SETS THE STAGE

The office in which a minister stands determines how we are to receive from him. If a minister is an evangelist, we receive from him differently than the way we receive from a teacher. The evangelist brings us a message of inspiration, causing us to sit on the edge of our seat, expecting a miracle to occur any minute.

Receiving a Ministry Gift

The teacher clearly and precisely unfolds the meaning of the Word to us. Revelation is growing line upon line as he ministers.

If the congregation does not accurately identify the office from which they are receiving ministry, it will be difficult for them to receive the most benefit. A further complication arises by not accurately identifying the office from which we are receiving. If believers do not understand the diversity of the function of the five offices, it is an easy trap for the enemy to tempt them into comparing ministers on the basis of personality, manner of delivery, or how he makes those receiving *"...feel..."*.

In the natural world we more easily accept the concept of diversity. There is even a familiar saying in the natural world that we must not compare apples to oranges. The meaning is clear. While we may like both apples and oranges, to compare one with the other will produce a wrong result. Apostles are different from prophets. Prophets are different from evangelists. Pastors are different from teachers. All five offices are different form one another or else Jesus would not have given different names to each of the five.

We get vitamin C from oranges and potassium from bananas. Understanding the diversity of the fruit keeps us from falsely comparing the two. Only a child, void of understanding, would dislike a banana because it is not juicy like the orange. Yet this mind-set seems to have crept in to the church on the earth and caused certain ministers to not be accepted by believers because he is not *"...like..."* some other minister. If the basis for making such a selection is a lack of understanding regarding diversity of ministry giftings, then we must grow in our understanding. We do not want to miss one single provision the Father has given for our growth and well-being.

SHEEP OF WOLF

How do we know whether to accept a minister as a man sent from God or a wolf sent by the enemy? There are three indicators which help us accept a minister as a man sent from God:

1. ***Recommendation from accepted minister.***

We see this indicator illustrated in the life and ministry of Apollos written about in scripture. Apollos decided to go in to Achaia,

> "...the brethren wrote, exhorting the disciples to receive him; and when arrived, he greatly helped those who had believed through grace; for he vigorously refuted the Jews publically, showing from the Scriptures that Jesus is the Christ..." **Acts 18:27,28**

Then, again, when Paul sent Timotheus to the Church in Corinth he writes,

> "Therefore I urge you, imitate me. For this reason I have sent Timothy to you, who is my believed and faithful son in the Lord, who will remind you of my ways in Christ, as I teach everywhere in every church."
> *I Corinthians 4:16,17*

Receiving a Ministry Gift

The most profound example of a personal recommendation for acceptance is in the case of Onesimus. Evidently, Onesimus had done something so that he was rejected by the Church in Archippus' house. Paul wrote to this church concerning their rejection.

> *"I appeal to you for my son Onesimus, whom I have begotten while in my chains, who once was unprofitable to you, but now is profitable to you and to me. I am sending him back. You therefore receive him, that is, my own heart."*
> **Philemon 1:10-12**

2. *Spiritual Perception.*

In the Old Testament we see this illustrated in the case of Elisha and the Shunamite woman.

> *"...And she said to her husband, "Look now, I know that this is a holy man of God, who passes by us regularly. Please, let us make a small upper room on the wall; and let us put a bed for him there, and a table and a chair and a lampstand; so it will be, whenever he comes to us, he can turn in there."* **II Kings 4:9,10**

Because of her *"...perception..."* she received Elisha as a man of God and built an addition onto their house to bless him. Her acceptance of him, based on perception, opened the door for the supernatural to be in operation in her life. Even though barren, she conceived a son supernaturally.

A New Testament example of this can be seen when the brethren at Jerusalem accepted Paul and Barnabas,

> "...and when James, Cephas, and John, who seemed to be pillars, perceived the grace that had been given to me, they gave me and Barnabas the right hand of fellowship, that we should go to the Gentiles and they to the circumcised." ***Galatians 2:9***

3. Doctrine.

> "Whoever transgresses and does not abide in the doctrine of Christ does not have God. He who abides in the doctrine of Christ has both the Father and the Son. If anyone comes to you and does not bring this doctrine, do not receive him into your house nor greet him; for he who greets him shares in his evil deeds."
> ***II John 9-11***

These three criteria will help us accept or reject a minister as a man of God. We accept or reject his ministry on the basis of confirmation from the Word and Spirit. Occasionally, a minister we have accepted delivers a message that does not line up with the Word. Because we have so totally accepted the minister, we do not bother to confirm his message through the Word and the Spirit. We simply accept it. This is how false doctrine or error begins to operate in the Church. No matter how much we accept a minister, we must always confirm his message through the Word and the Spirit.

On the other hand, occasionally, ministers who are really ministers of God, but whom we do not accept for some reason, bring us powerful revelation from the Word. Because we do not accept the minister, we reject their message. This is a case of hard-hearted carnal mindedness on those who receive. God used Balaam's donkey to deliver a divine message. We must be sensitive to accept God's ministers and God's message as He gives them to the Church. It is quite often simply our lack of acceptance of either God's ministers or God's message that causes division in the Church, rather than heresy or false doctrine.

The only way the saints are going to accurately identify the offices of ministry and know the ministry each office has for the Church is if they are properly taught on the offices and if there is proper demonstration of each ministry gift.

DEMONSTRATION OF EACH MINISTRY GIFT

Right now there are many men and women walking in these five offices with supernatural credentials of God's confirmation on their calling. The time has come for us to begin to recognize the gift operating in these people's lives and receive them as apostles, prophets, evangelists, pastors, and teachers. When we receive persons who are truly called by God to stand in each of these five offices, we will begin to see greater demonstrations of each office. We must receive a prophet as a prophet in order to receive a prophet's reward.

The circle of acceptance must grow larger than just an inner circle among ministers only. It is when the saints who fill the pews acknowledge and accept and receive the five offices that we will truly see the supernatural ministry of these five offices flourish again.

There are four components necessary for the door to be opened to unlimited supernatural ministry: The *"...minister..."* must...

1. Acknowledge, and

2. Accept the office to which he has been called, and the *"...congregation..."* must...

3. Acknowledge, and

4. Accept the five offices of ministry and ministers standing in these offices.

When these four things are present, we will see demonstration of the ministry gifts on a more consistent basis than we do today.

Chapter Seven
DEFINING THE GIFTS

For the saints to acknowledge and accept the five gifts of ministry of apostle, prophet, evangelist, pastor, and teacher in a greater way, we are going to need a more expanded view of each office. Our previous understanding of each office was so narrow we really did not see each gift in a practical way directly affecting the saints' perfection or the Church's unity.

Because the New Testament was written in the Greek language, the terms apostle, prophet, evangelist, pastor, and teacher were all terms used among the Greeks before they became terms used to identify gifts given by Christ. The Greeks used these terms in ways not related to the Church of the Lord Jesus. Each term had a Greek definition or meaning associated with it. However, we cannot use the Greek definition alone to get an accurate understanding of God's supernaturally given ministry gifts.

Considering another term used by both the Greeks and the Church will help us to see the challenges associated with pre-Church Greek usage of a term before we begin to consider the five offices of ministry. The Greek term *"...ekkleesia..."* is generally translated in the New Testament as *"...church...".* It is hard for us to imagine this term ever meaning anything but the Church of the Lord Jesus. However, the Greeks used the term to refer to *"...a calling out, for example, a popular meeting...".*

Temple of Glory

In Ephesus a silversmith named Demetrius, who made shrines of the goddess Diana, called other workmen of the same trade together and began to complain about Paul. Paul had great results in Ephesus and throughout all Asia bringing many people to Christ. This meant the new believers would no longer need silver shrines of the goddess Diana. Therefore, Paul was bad for the shrine business.

Demetrius stirred up these silver craftsmen. A crowd gathered to consider these matters and the whole city was filled with confusion as a result. They even caught Gaius and Aristarchus, men of Macedonia who were Paul's companions in travel.

> *"Some therefore cried one thing and some another, for the **assembly** was confused, and most of them did not know why they had come together."* **Acts 19:32**

The town clerk quieted the crowd and told them,

> *"...if you have any other inquiry to make, it shall be determined in the lawful **assembly**. For we are in danger of being called in question for today's uproar, there being no reason which we may give to account for this disorderly gathering. And when he had said these things, he dismissed the **assembly**."* **Acts 19:39-41**

All three places using the English term *"...assembly..."* was translated as such from the original Greek term *"...ekkleesia..."*. The people of Ephesus in this incident were *"...called out..."* as one gathering for one purpose, to discuss Paul's Christianity in relation to the goddess Diana.

Defining the Gifts

It is the same with the Greek definition of each of the five terms apostle, prophet, evangelist, pastor, and teacher. In order to complete the definition of each of these terms as God's supernaturally called gifts given to the Church, we must turn to the Word and the Spirit.

Typically, the narrowly accepted definition for these terms has been: apostles start churches; prophets prophesy; evangelists win the lost; pastors shepherd the local flock; and teachers teach topics from the Word. These definitions are too narrow to really understand what God has given the Church. In order to more clearly define, even in principle, these five offices we must reconsider their purpose for being given.

> "...For the equipping of the saints, for the work of ministry, for the edifying of the body of Christ..."
> ***Ephesians 4:12***

This purpose is amplified in the next verse. The amplification presents two real keys which help open the door to a clearer view of each office.

> "...till we all come to the unity of the faith and of the knowledge of the Son of God, to a perfect man, to the measure of the stature of the fullness of Christ..."
> ***Ephesians 4:13***

The two key statements within this verse are:

1. "...*Knowledge of the Son of God...*", and

2. "...*Unto a perfect man...*".

Perfecting the saints is bringing Christians to maturity. Bringing Christians to maturity is having Christ formed in them. Christ is formed in them through the impartation and receiving of *"...revelation knowledge..."*. This revelation knowledge is Christ being revealed. The main component which causes us to be perfected and unified is our knowledge of the Son of God. We have already seen our knowledge of the Son of God is not simply knowing about Him, but rather knowing Him. The more intimate our relationship with God becomes, the more of His kind of life will be manifest in us.

Each office relates to Jesus from the perspective of their particular calling. For example, the evangelist sees Jesus as the Savior of the world. The teacher sees Jesus as the Word to be explained to the saints. Each of the five offices impart knowledge of certain aspects of the Son of God according to their calling. Maybe we could say this another way, each office of ministry sees Jesus from the unique perspective of their individual calling, and impart that knowledge to the sons of God as the means for their spiritual growth.

Scripture clearly states the goal is *"...unto a perfect man..."* While we desire to see all of the sons of God perfected and doing the works of Jesus here on the earth, our ultimate goal is not many perfect men, but rather one perfect man. All newly born again believers were immediately baptized into Christ and became the many membered flesh and bone body of Christ in the earth. Our ultimate goal is that the world may know the Father sent Jesus as a direct result of

Defining the Gifts

the unity of the brethren. Christ was commissioned to build the Temple of the Lord, a single identifiable building. This building is Christ on the earth. Each person called to one of the five offices of ministry must keep this goal at the forefront of his purpose of ministry.

> *"...speaking the truth in love, may grow up in all things into Him who is the head, Christ, from whom the whole body, joined and knit together by what every joint supplies, according to the effective working by which every part does its share, causes growth of the body for the edifying of itself in love."* **Ephesians 4:15,16**

Part of our expanded definition for these five offices will include these two things:

1. Each office imparts revelation knowledge of the Son of God from the unique perspective of their calling in order to help perfect the saints.

2. Each office helps motivate the saints with the goal of producing a *"...perfect man..."* as one Temple of the Lord.

But what exactly does each of the five offices do? What responsibilities does each have in the building process?

Answers will be built on the foundation of what we already know:

1. The five offices have been given as supernatural personnel by God to help the commission be fulfilled.

2. The commission is to build the Temple of the Lord.

3. Building the Temple is one building project with many different components of construction.

4. No one component is more important than any of the other components.

5. Christ is the head of the Church and director of all supernatural personnel.

Each of the five offices have been given specific responsibilities, just like builders on a construction site. Jesus is the general contractor and each departmental foreman relates to Him as overseer. Each department must also relate to other departments in the building process, otherwise the building could not be built correctly. The man who lays foundation on a natural construction site must relate to the plumber so the plumber can lay some of his plumbing before the foundation is poured. The carpenters must relate to the electrician so the electrician can install the wiring before the walls are covered. All of the construction workers must relate to one another on a construction site in order to build correctly.

Defining the Gifts

The definition of each office is going to be the same thing as *"...determining responsibilities..."* for each office in relation to building the Temple of the Lord. This type of *"...building..."* mind-set will help achieve the comprehensive view needed for each office. In order to build a building we need trained and equipped builders to be responsible for each component of construction. Scripture has identified these builders as apostles, prophets, evangelists, pastors, and teachers.

Successful construction is only possible on a natural building if the the construction site is *"...cleared..."*: Underbrush must be cut away, hindering obstacles must be removed, hills leveled, and valleys filled. So, too, successful spiritual construction requires a clear site. The thief who only comes to steal, kill, and destroy will employ his devices in an effort to hinder the construction process. Intercession is essential to keep strongholds pulled down, battle principalities, powers, rulers of the darkness of this world, and spiritual wickedness in high places. ***Intercession is a required companion in building the Temple of the Lord.***

In order to begin construction we must have building materials. The office God has given to gather spiritual materials with which to build is the office of evangelist.

EVANGELIST

In the pre-Christian Greek world, even though rarely used, this term *"...uangelistees..."* meant one who proclaimed authoritative or wise sayings. It is also used rarely in the

New Testament, only three times. The meaning is similarly defined as *"...one who proclaims glad tidings..."*.

The three uses of the term *"...evangelist..."* in the New Testament are:

1. *"...and some, evangelists..."* **Ephesians 4:11**, listed as one of the gifts Christ has given to men.

2. Paul's exhortation Timothy to *"...do the work of an evangelist..."* **II Timothy 4:5**.

3. Luke writing of *"...Philip the evangelist..."*
Acts 21:8.

Because the term is used in the *Ephesians* context as a gift of Christ, we know the office has a specific function. Christ's gifts are always functional. This is confirmed in the *Timothy* reference, when Paul told Timothy to do *"...the work of an evangelist..."*. In order for Timothy to do the work of an evangelist, he would have to know what work the evangelist did. There is not enough information from only three scripture references to learn what work the evangelist does.

Luke's use of the term *"...evangelist..."* in application to Philip allows us to follow the life and ministry of Philip to see the office in manifestation. While examining Philip's ministry we must guard against defining the office exclusively on the basis of what Philip did or of making his ministry the prototype for all evangelist's ministries. Rather, Philip's minis-

Defining the Gifts

try will provide an *"in-principle..."* illustration of the office. For example, Luke wrote the angel of the Lord directed Philip to the road which led south to Gaza. On this road Philip found a chariot carrying an Ethiopian Eunuch. Philip was instructed by the Lord to join himself to this chariot. As soon as Philip entered into the chariot, he began to preach Christ. Philip's preaching of Christ led the Eunuch to receive Jesus as his personal Lord and Savior. Upon his proclamation of faith, the Eunuch stopped the chariot at the first place of water for Philip to baptize him. Immediately, following the baptism, Philip was caught away to another location by the Spirit of the Lord. Philip was *"...trans-located..."*.

If we use Philip as the prototypical evangelist for all persons called to the office of evangelist and follow the old pattern of defining a ministry gift on the basis of what a minister does, then we would have to say that one of the acts defining a true New Testament evangelist would be *"trans-location"*. It is easy to see that this type of defining process will lead us astray. Trans-location is not a qualification for a person to be an evangelist, just as being shipwrecked is not a qualification for a person to be an apostle. Trans-location in Philip's life and ministry was merely one isolated incident on the journey of his ministry, just as the shipwreck was only one isolated incident on the journey of Paul's ministry.

However, we can use this Ethiopian Eunuch illustration in Philip's ministry to see *"...in-principle..."* the office of evangelist. This ministry account of Philip and the Eunuch began with the angel of the Lord sending Philip to the Gaza road on a mission. Why was Philip sent? He was already involved in ministry in the city of Samaria producing tremendous fruit. Yet the Lord took Philip out of this setting to send him to the Eunuch. What was the specific mission on which the Lord was sending him?

Luke wrote the Ethiopian had been to Jerusalem to worship God. He also wrote the Eunuch was reading from the scroll of the Prophet Isaiah. After Philip had joined himself to the chariot, the Eunuch asked Philip about the prophet's writings. This Ethiopian man was hungering to know God! He was seeking the kingdom of God. Luke wrote,

> "...For everyone who asks receives, and he who seeks finds, and to him who knocks it will be opened..."
> **Luke 11:10**

The Ethiopian met these requirements of asking, seeking, and knocking in order to find God. The Lord was responding by sending him a specialist in proclaiming glad tidings of good things, an *"...evangelist..."*!

Philip was sent to preach Christ to the Ethiopian so the Eunuch could hear, believe, and be saved. Paul wrote a beautiful summary of the evangelist's ministry to the lost in his letter to the saints in Rome. He wrote,

> "For whoever calls on the name of the Lord shall be saved. How then shall they call on Him in whom they have not believed? And how shall they believe in Him of whom they have not heard? And how shall they hear

Defining the Gifts

without a preacher? As it is written: "How beautiful are the feet of those who preach the gospel of peace, who bring glad tidings of good things!"
Romans 10:13-15

The evangelist's ministry to the saints is to impart revelation of Jesus as Savior for all men everywhere. This revelation, burning within the evangelist, creates a zeal within him for the lost to know Jesus. When he ministers to the saints this zeal is imparted to them so they receive clear understanding of the heart of Jesus for the world to be saved. This aspect of knowledge of the Son of God comes through most strongly from the evangelist.

EVANGELIST DEFINED

In-principle, then, the office of evangelist can be defined as a supernatural gatherer of stones to serve as building materials necessary to build the Temple of the Lord. He fulfills the responsibilities of his office by ministering revelation of Jesus as Savior to the lost and to the saints. The revelation ministered to the lost is for them to accept Jesus. The revelation ministered to the saints is for them to present Jesus to the world.

The evangelist ministers to the lost as non-believers, meaning they have not yet begun their walk of faith. We know it is by grace through faith that we are saved. Therefore, all Christians are believers, but the lost have not yet believed. Because all lost do not yet believe, the evangelist needs special credibility for them to receive him as a messenger bringing salvation from the true and living God. This special credibility is in two forms:

Temple of Glory

1. Special manifestation of the Holy Spirit's ministry to the lost.

2. Signs and miracles.

Jesus explained how the Holy Spirit ministers to the lost,

> "...*He will convict the world of sin, and of righteousness, and of judgment: of sin, because they do not believe in Me; of righteousness, because I go to My Father and you see Me no more; of judgment, because the ruler of this world is judged...*" ***John 16:8-11***

The evangelist proclaims glad tidings of Jesus as redeemer and the Holy Spirit convinces those who have "...*ears to hear...*" the message to accept Christ as Savior.

Luke wrote about signs and miracles regarding Philip's ministry,

> "*Then Philip went down to the city of Samaria and preached Christ to them. And the multitudes with one accord heeded the things spoken by Philip, hearing and seeing the miracles which he did. For unclean spirits, crying with a loud voice, came out of many who were possessed; and many who were paralyzed and lame were healed. And there was great joy in that city.*"
> ***Acts 8:5-8***

It is important to remember is not the signs and miracles which make a person an evangelist. Nor is it the gathering of living stones. Every believer is to do the works of Jesus which includes signs and miracles. Every believer is to be a minister of reconciliation, which is winning the lost.

Defining the Gifts

What makes a person an evangelist is the call of God.

A person may be an evangelist called of God and gather many living stones without signs and miracles. Signs and miracles simply provide special credibility for the evangelist as he ministers to non-believers.

After building materials have been gathered, construction can begin. The first component of construction is laying the foundation in the new believers. The offices God has given as foundation layers are apostle and prophet.

APOSTLE

The occasional non-Christian use of this term *"...apostolos..."* by the Greeks was as a naval term in sea-going ventures. The fleet of military ships sent on an expedition and the admiral in charge were both referred to by this Greek term. The general meaning of the term was *"...a delegate sent out..."*. In the New Testament, **Strong's Exhaustive Concordance of the Bible** defines the term (# 652) as,

> *"...a delegate, specifically an ambassador of the gospel; officially a commissioner of Christ."*

Matthew uses the term to refer to the twelve disciples who walked with Jesus on the earth.

> *"Now the names of the twelve apostles are these: first, Simon, who is called Peter, and Andrew his brother; James the son of Zebedee, and John his brother; Philip and*

Temple of Glory

Bartholomew; Thomas and Matthew the tax collector; James the son of Alphaeus, and Lebbaeus, whose surname was Thaddeus; Simon the Cananite, and Judas Iscariot, who also betrayed Him." **Matthew 10:2-4**

Judas who was numbered with the twelve betrayed Jesus then...

"...purchased a field with the wages of iniquity; and falling headlong, he burst open in the middle and all his entrails gushed out." **Acts 1:18**

King David prophesied about Judas in Psalms as Peter tells us,

"For as it is written in the Book of Psalms: 'Let his dwelling place be desolate, and let no one live in it'; and, 'Let another take his office.'" **Acts 1:20**

After Judas died another person was ordained to walk together with the eleven as one of the apostles. Sometime before the day of Pentecost when the believers were together in the upper room, Peter spoke to the brethren about the need to replace Judas. He said,

"Therefore, of these men who have accompanied us all the time that the Lord Jesus went in and out among us, beginning from the baptism of John to that day when He was taken up from us, one of these must become a witness with us of His resurrection..." **Acts 1:21,22**

Matthias was ordained to take Judas' place and,

"...he was numbered with the eleven apostles." **Acts 1:26**

Once again there were twelve apostles.

Defining the Gifts

John wrote of these twelve apostles in the book of Revelation. He said of an angel,

> *"And he carried me away in the spirit to a great and high mountain, and showed me the great city, the holy Jerusalem, descending out of heaven from God...Now the wall of the city had twelve foundations, and on them were the names of the twelve apostles of the Lamb."* **Revelation 21:10,14**

These twelve called *"...Apostles of the Lamb..."*, whose names are written on the twelve foundations of the wall of new Jerusalem, are a special closed group of apostles. No one could ever be an apostle in the same sense as these twelve men because of two facts:

    1. They were companied together with Jesus all the time during Jesus' earthly ministry.

    2. The Lord has chosen their names to be written in the foundation of the wall of new Jerusalem.

However, we do see others called apostles in the New Testament. Two of the best known are

> *"...the apostles, Barnabas and Paul..."* **Acts 14:14**

Another is spoken of by Paul when he went up to Jerusalem to see Peter,

> *"...but I saw none of the other apostles except James, the Lord's brother."* **Galatians 1:19**

These used of the term *"...apostolos"* referring to Paul, Barnabas, and James the son of Joseph help our understanding to see the term was not limited to the original twelve apostles of the Lamb.

All of these men who were called apostles in the New Testament are dead. Is there evidence the office of apostle still exists as a functional office today? There is conclusive evidence the term apostle is still to be used to refer to gifts of ministry in the Church today. The evidence is found in Paul's letter to the Church at Ephesus.

Paul said the five gifts of apostle, prophet, evangelist, pastor, and teacher have been given for the perfecting of the saints, for the work of the ministry, for the edifying of the Body of Christ,

> *"...till we all come to the unity of the faith and of the knowledge of the Son of God, to a perfect man, to the measure of the stature of the fullness of Christ..."* **Ephesians 4:13**

We have not all come into the unity of the faith nor of the knowledge of the Son of God unto a perfect man. All five gifts have been given until we achieve these expectations of God. Therefore, if we acknowledge the ministries of evangelist, pastor, and teacher as gifts from Christ for today, then we must also acknowledge the present day ministries of apostle and prophet as gifts from Christ for today.

> *"The gifts and callings of God are irrevocable."*
> **Romans 11:29**

We see the term *"...apostolos..."* translated *"...apostle..."* can still be used today to identify a ministry gift of Christ within the Church. But what about an accurate definition for the term?

Defining the Gifts

What is the function of an apostle? Those who accept the contemporary function of the office have commonly accepted the definition of *"...apostle..."* as a term used to identify the ministry gift who starts churches. Does this correctly identify the responsibilities of the office of apostle according to the Word? Our definition needs to be according to the Word and the Spirit, not according to the traditional understanding of the ministry gift or the non-Christian Greek definition.

Paul seems to be the most known of the New Testament apostles by the modern day Church. It will be easy, then, to use Paul's ministry as example of the office of apostle. There is no doubt Paul, formerly known as Saul of Tarsus, was an apostle. He opened nine of the letters he wrote to various Churches by identifying himself as Paul, an apostle of Jesus Christ. He further qualified his calling by saying he was an apostle by the will of God, not by man.

The Church at Corinth was having many internal difficulties. Paul's first letter to them was primarily written to address these problems. In the third chapter he deals with carnal attitudes regarding politics within the Church. There were divisions among the saints,

> *"...For when one says, "I am of Paul," and another, "I am of Apollos," are you not carnal?..."* **I Corinthians 3:4**

Paul explained to them these ministers were merely men by whom they believed, even as the Lord gave to every man. He said one minister plants and another waters, but it is God who gives the increase. He called the Church God's husbandry and God's building. Then Paul made clear what part he had played in the Corinthian's lives.

Temple of Glory

> *"According to the grace of God which was given to me, as a wise master builder I have laid the foundation, and another builds on it. But let each one take heed how he builds on it."* ***I Corinthians 3:10***

Paul was the ministry gift who laid the foundation for the Corinthian's lives as Christians.

Was this foundational ministry unique to Paul and the believers at Corinth because he had pioneered this Church? Paul wrote,

> *"For though you might have ten thousand instructors in Christ, yet you do not have many fathers; for in Christ Jesus I have begotten you through the gospel."*
> ***I Corinthians 4:15***

Did Paul lay the foundation in these believers' lives simply because he had led them into the new birth? Or was it because he was the only minister available to lay the foundation after their new birth? Or did he lay the foundation because he was an apostle? The second and third chapters of Paul's letters to the Ephesians provide answers to these questions.

> *"Now, therefore, you are no longer strangers and foreigners, but fellow citizens with the saints and members of the household of God, having been built on the foundation of the apostles and prophets, Jesus Christ Himself being the chief cornerstone..."* ***Ephesians 2:19,20***

Paul is writing here to the Gentiles who had become believers in Ephesus. He said these Gentile believers were built upon the foundation of the apostles and prophets with Jesus Himself as the chief cornerstone. What was this foundation and how was it laid?

Defining the Gifts

In a verbal exchange Jesus had with His disciples, He asked them who they thought He was. Peter answered,

> *"You are the Christ, the Son of the living God. Jesus answered and said to him, "Blessed are you, Simon Bar-Jonah, for flesh and blood has not revealed this to you, but My Father who is in heaven. And I also say to you that you are Peter, and on this rock I will build My church, and the gates of Hades shall not prevail against it."* **Matthew 16:16-18**

Jesus pronounced to His disciples and to as many as believe in future generations that Peter's answer was a ***"...divine revelation of the Christ..."***. Then, He expanded His answer to say that upon this divine revelation He, Jesus, would build His church.

Jesus was absolutely not saying Peter was going to be the foundation of the church Jesus was going to build. God the Holy Spirit inspired the apostle Paul to write specifically about the foundation of the church,

> *"For no other foundation can anyone lay than that which is laid, which is Jesus Christ."* **I Corinthians 3:11**

Isaiah the prophet speaking by divine inspiration prophesied about the foundation of the church which was to come,

> *"Therefore thus says the Lord God: "Behold, I lay in Zion a stone for a foundation, a tried stone, a precious cornerstone, a sure foundation: whoever believes will not act hastily."*
> **Isaiah 28:16**

Jesus is this precious cornerstone and sure foundation on which the church is being built.

Temple of Glory

The foundation upon which the Gentile believers were built was this revelation of Jesus as the Christ, the Son of God. Paul said their foundation was the work of the apostles and prophets. In other words, the apostles and prophets brought these Gentiles into a revelation of Christ. Then how does the work of these foundation layers differ from the work of the evangelist, who also brings people into the saving knowledge of Jesus as the Christ, the Son of God, and Savior of the world?

The apostle Peter's writings to new believers distinguishes between the ministry of the evangelist and the ministries of the apostle and the prophet.

> "...As newborn babes, desire the pure milk of the word, that you may grow thereby, if indeed you have tasted that the Lord is gracious." **I Peter 2:2,3**

The newborn babe in Christ has only "...*tasted*..." the Lord's grace. The new believer needs more than just a taste in order to grow and be established so the gates of Hades will not prevail against him. Peter shows us the taste the new believers have received,

> "Therefore it is also contained in Scripture, "Behold, I lay in Zion a chief cornerstone, elect, precious, and he who believes on Him will by no means be put to shame."
> **I Peter 2:6**

The initial "...*taste of the Lord*..." the new believer receives is revelation of the "...*chief cornerstone*..." of the foundation, the revelation that Jesus is Lord.

Defining the Gifts

Paul wrote to the church at Rome about the means to be saved,

> *"...if you confess with your mouth the Lord Jesus and believe in your heart that God has raised Him from the dead, you will be saved..."* **Romans 10:9**

The revelation a person must hear in order to be saved is minimal, just a *"...cornerstone of the foundation..."*. The revelation of Jesus the believer needs to receive in order to have a complete foundation on which his whole Christian life can be built is more than just the cornerstone of the foundation received at the time of his new birth.

The Holy Spirit has inspired various writers in the Bible to use the term *"...cornerstone..."*. When a building was built in both Old Testament and New Testament times the foundation required a cornerstone to be laid. This stone was a single stone cut with precision and set at one corner of the foundation of the building. All measurements to keep the building square and according to building specifications were oriented to the cornerstone. Although the cornerstone had particular importance in the building process, it was not the entire foundation, nor was it the entire building. It was only one very important but small part of the whole building.

The evangelist lays the chief cornerstone of the foundation and the apostle and prophet complete the foundation. The completed foundation will cause the believer to be established. In closing his letter to the saints at Rome Paul wrote,

Temple of Glory

> *"...Now to Him who is able to establish you according to my gospel and the preaching of Jesus Christ, according to the revelation of the mystery kept secret since the world began..."* **Romans 16:25**

Paul is preaching Jesus Christ. Paul has already written that Jesus Christ is the only foundation that can be laid. Jesus is both the cornerstone of the foundation and the entire foundation of the church.

The mystery Paul preached, *"...Christ in you, the hope of glory..."*, and all that it entails is the complete foundation which will cause the believer's Christian life to be established so he can grow into the temple God intended for him to be and to keep the gates of Hades from prevailing against him. God has chosen apostles and prophets to lay this foundation.

APOSTLE DEFINED

In principle, then, the office of apostle can be defined as a foundation layer. He completes the foundational revelation of Jesus, of which the evangelist laid the cornerstone. The sign of an apostle is not how many Churches he has started but rather how many he has established on a sure foundation. There are many churches already started today which are not established. They need the foundational ministries of the apostle and the prophet.

Paul defined his own ministry in his letter to the church at Ephesus,

Defining the Gifts

"For this reason I, Paul, the prisoner of Christ Jesus for you Gentiles, if indeed you have heard of the dispensation of the grace of God which was given to me for you, how that by revelation He made known to me the mystery (as I have briefly written already, by which, when you read, you may understand my knowledge in the mystery of Christ), which in other ages was not made known to the sons of men, as it has now been revealed by the Spirit to His holy apostles and prophets; that the Gentiles should be fellow heirs, of the same body, and partakers of His promise in Christ through the gospel, of which I became a minister according to the gift of the grace of God given to me by the effective working of His power." **Ephesians 3:1-7**

At first reading it appears the mystery Paul preached was *"...that the Gentiles should be fellow heirs, of the same body, and partakers of His promise in Christ through the gospel...".* However, the mystery Paul preached ws not the Gentiles in Christ, but rather, Christ in the Gentiles, and in all men who believe on Him. The following four scripture references together provide a summary of Paul's knowledge of the mystery.

➤ *"There is neither Jew nor Greek, there is neither slave nor free, there is neither male nor female; for you are all one in Christ Jesus."* **Galatians 3:28**

➤ *"That in the dispensation of the fullness of the times He might gather together in one all things in Christ, both which are in heaven and which are on earth in Him."*
Ephesians 1:10

➤ *"For we are members of His body, of His flesh and of His bones. For this reason a man shall leave his father and mother and be joined to his wife, and the two shall become one flesh. This is a great mystery, but I speak concerning Christ and the church."* **Ephesians 5:30-32**

Temple of Glory

> *"To whom God would make known what is the riches of the glory of this mystery among the Gentiles: which is Christ in you, the hope of glory."* **Colossians 1:27**

This mystery of Christ and the Church is revealed to the apostles and prophets and ministered by them as foundation for each individual believer, and for the corporate Church. Paul wrote,

> *"...(the saints are) built upon the foundation of the apostles and prophets, Jesus Christ Himself being the chief cornerstone, in whom the whole building, being fitted together, grows into a holy temple in the Lord..."*
> **Ephesians 2:20,21**

PROPHET

Kittel Theological Dictionary speaks of the Greek use of the term *"...propheetees..."*: It simply expresses the formal function of declaring, proclaiming, making known. When the term appeared in the literature of the fifth century, it already had a broad use for the oracle prophet, for the poet, and over a wider sphere not only for persons, but also, by poetic transference for *"...things..."*.

"There can be no doubt that *"...propheetees..."* belongs to the religious sphere, where it denotes the one who speaks in the name of a god, declaring divine will and counsel in the oracle." **Kittel Theological Dictionary,** Volume VI, page 795.

Defining the Gifts

The New Testament use of the term is parallel in meaning to that found in Kittel. It is defined by most authoritative works simply as a proclaimer of a divinely inspired message.

The Holy Spirit has already informed us that apostles and prophets are both foundation layers as Paul wrote the Gentile believers in Ephesus were,

> *"...built on the foundation of the apostles and prophets, Jesus Christ Himself being the chief cornerstone..."*
> **Ephesians 2:20**

While similar, we also know there is enough difference between the two offices for Christ Jesus to have separated them into two distinct offices, and referring to one as *"...apostle..."* and the other as *"...prophet...".* They are both foundational ministry gifts, but separate terms are required in order to identify the differences between the two offices.

In the natural world we have many such separations between things in the same class. For example, in the class of vehicles, a bus and a car are both classed vehicles with the same general function. They both transport passengers and cargo. However, there are enough differences between the two that we must use separate terms to help us identify the differences between the two vehicles. Even though there are many similarities in the function of both vehicles, it is easy for us to identify the differences between a bus and a car. Identification is made simply by clearly defining each vehicle.

Even though there are similar functions of both offices of apostle and prophet, we can still define in-principle the differences between the two offices in order to help identify each office. Jesus has already written about the need to receive a prophet's reward, we must receive a prophet as a prophet. In order to receive a prophet as a prophet, we must know *"...what..."* and *"...who..."* a prophet is.

Because the non-Christian Greek definition will not accurately define this supernatural office of ministry given by God, we must turn again to the Word and the Spirit. Using the life and ministry of a man identified as a prophet in the New Testament will help achieve the necessary insights to help properly define in-principle the office of prophet.

In the eleventh and twenty-first chapters of the book of Acts, Luke writes about a man named Agabus.

> *"And in these days prophets came from Jerusalem to Antioch. Then one of them, named Agabus, stood up and showed by the Spirit that there was going to be a great famine throughout all the world, which also happened in the days of Claudius Caesar. Then the disciples, each according to his ability, determined to send relief to the brethren dwelling in Judaea. This they also did, and sent it to the elders by the hands of Barnabas and Saul."* **Acts 11:27-30**

There is another account of this prophetic ministry recorded by Luke in another portion of his letter which adds information to help our understanding. Luke writes that Paul and his company traveled to Caesarea to the house of Philip the evangelist.

Defining the Gifts

> *"And as we stayed many days, a certain prophet named Agabus came down from Judea. When he had come to us, he took Paul's belt, bound his own hands and feet, and said, "Thus says the Holy Spirit, 'So shall the Jews at Jerusalem bind the man who owns this belt, and deliver him into the hands of the Gentiles."* **Acts 21:10,11**

In the first account Luke writes that Agabus, *"...signified by the Spirit..."*. In the second account Luke wrote that Agabas said, *"...thus says the Holy Spirit..."*. In both accounts Agabus was *"...the proclaimer of a divinely inspired message..."*. The nature of both divinely inspired messages was future oriented: Declaring a coming dearth throughout the entire world and the imprisonment of Paul in Jerusalem. The context of both divinely inspired messages was such that advance preparations could be made regarding future events. In the first account regarding the coming dearth throughout the whole world, the disciples who received the prophet's ministry sent financial relief to the brethren in Judaea. In the second account of Paul's future imprisonment, Paul could have changed plans and avoided imprisonment, but he believed it was the Lord's will for him to go to Jerusalem.

These ministry accounts of Agabus as a prophet do not show the foundational aspect of the prophet's ministry. However, they do help identify a vital aspect of the New Testament prophet: *"...seeing..."* by the power of the Spirit of God. In the Old Testament in the book of Samuel it is written:

> *"Formerly in Israel, when a man went to inquire of God, he spoke thus: "Come, let us go to the seer"; for he who is now called a prophet was formerly called a seer."*
> **I Samuel 9:9**

Temple of Glory

This *"...seeing..."* was both forward into the future and backward into the past.

The prophet Samuel was also called *"...Samuel the seer..."* **I Chronicles 29:29.** Samuel's ministry as *"...seer..."* looked both into the future and into the past, as demonstrated in his relationship with Saul.

> *"Now the Lord had told Samuel in his ear the day before Saul came, saying, "Tomorrow about this time I will send you a man from the Land of Benjamin, and you shall anoint him commander over My people Israel, that he may save My people from the hand of the Philistines; for I have looked upon My people, because their cry has come to Me."* **I Samuel 9:15,16**

Here the Lord is allowing Samuel to *"...see..."* into the future to know who will be King over Israel, and to *"...see..."* the Israelites will be saved from the Philistines.

When Saul came near to Samuel asking the location of the *"...seer's..."* house Samuel answered him saying,

> *"I am the seer. Go up before me to the high place, for you shall eat with me today; and tomorrow I will let you go and will tell you all that is in your heart. But as for your donkeys that were lost three days ago, do not be anxious about them, for they have been found. And on whom is all the desire of Israel? Is it not on you and on all your father's house?"* **I Samuel 9:19,20**

Samuel *"...seeing..."* by the power of the Spirit of the Lord, saw the *"...past..."* regarding the lost donkeys, and about Saul's heart.

Defining the Gifts

PROPHET DEFINED

As a prophet in the New Testament, Agabus illustrates the "...seeing..." aspect of the office of prophet as demonstrated in the Old Testament. This will be the major factor used to define the office of prophet as distinct from that of apostle. In-principle, then, the New Testament prophet is a "...seer..." as well as a foundational ministry gift. By divine inspiration and initiation he "...sees..." events in the spirit realm and relates those events to man in the natural realm. Just as the office of apostle receives divine revelation concerning the mystery of Christ and the Church, so, too, the office of prophet receives divine revelation concerning the mystery of Christ and the Church. The revelation both the apostle and the prophet receive serve as foundation for the individual believer and for the corporate church.

PASTOR

During the time period of history immediately before Christ and just after His earthly life and ministry, agriculture and cattle were basic to the economy in the middle east. The Greek term from which the English term *"...pastor..."* is translated is *"...poimen..."*. This Greek term was a commonly used term to identify what we refer to in English as a *"...shepherd..."*. In the account of Jesus' birth, Luke wrote about,

> *"Now there were in the same country shepherds living out in the fields, keeping watch over their flock by night."*
> **Luke 2:8**

These shepherds were the same as what you and I call shepherds today. Their clothes were different from the shepherds' clothes of today, and their tools were not as sophisticated as shepherds use today, but their basic function was the same: *tend flocks of sheep*. In the New Testament in his letter to the church at Ephesus, Paul used the term *"...poimen..."* to identify an office of ministry given by Christ. The term *"...poimen..."* Paul used is the same term used by Luke to identify shepherds tending flocks of sheep. It is obvious additional information is required to be able to understand how *"...poimen..."* can be used in a spiritual sense to identify an office of ministry given by Christ and natural shepherds.

Specific people standing in other offices of ministry have been identified with the appropriate Greek term. For example, *"...Philip the evangelist..."*; or *"...the apostles, Barnabas and Paul..."*; or *"...a certain prophet, named Agabus..."*. However, there are no examples of a particular New Testament person identified as, *"...pastor so-n-so..."*. Because there are no specific examples of a particular individual as pastor, it is more difficult to illustrate this office of ministry from the Word as we have done for evangelist, apostle, and prophet. Therefore, indirect examples will be required to illustrate this ministry gift.

Because the Holy Spirit inspired the use of the term *"...poimen..."* to identify this office of ministry, we can conclude the spiritual function of the office will be similar to the natural function of the shepherd who tends flocks. King David was a shepherd as a boy in the Old Testament. Even though his story was told in Hebrew and not Greek, David is still an excellent illustration from the Word to help promote understanding of the function of shepherd.

Defining the Gifts

The Lord sent the prophet Samuel to anoint one of Jesse the Bethlehemite's sons to be king over Israel.

> *"...Thus Jesse made seven of his sons pass before Samuel. And Samuel said to Jesse, "The Lord has not chosen these." And Samuel said to Jesse, "Are all the young men here?" Then he said, "There remains yet the youngest, and there he is keeping the sheep." And Samuel said to Jesse, "Send and bring him. For we will not sit down till he comes here."* **I Samuel 16:10,11**

This was David. David, the shepherd, was not in his father's house with the rest of his family because he stayed with the sheep. This is one of the first things we see about the shepherd: ***He stays with the sheep.***

David was anointed by Samuel. Sometime later David was summoned to play his harp to quiet the troubled King Saul. David came and played for Saul. Then it is recorded,

> *"...David occasionally went and returned from Saul to feed his father's sheep at Bethlehem."* **I Samuel 17:15**

Part of David's shepherding responsibility was to feed the sheep.

Then, during the war with the Philistines, David vowed to defeat Goliath. He was brought before Saul where he gave account of why he should be allowed to fight the giant Goliath.

> *"But David said to Saul, "Your servant used to keep his father's sheep, and when a lion or a bear came and took a lamb out of the flock, I went out after it and struck it,*

and delivered the lamb from its mouth; and when it arose against me, I caught it by its beard, and struck and killed it. Your servant has killed both lion and bear; and this uncircumcised Philistine will be like one of them, seeing he has defied the armies of the living God."
                                       I Samuel 17:34-36

Here David demonstrates yet another aspect of the shepherd's duties: ***Guarding the flock against danger.***

In the Psalms David wrote,

"The Lord is my shepherd; I shall not want. He makes me to lie down in green pastures; He leads me beside the still waters. He restores my soul; He leads me in the paths of righteousness for His name's sake. Yea, though I walk through the valley of the shadow of death, I will fear no evil; for You are with me; Your rod and Your staff, they comfort me. You prepare a table before me in the presence of my enemies; You anoint my head with oil; my cup runs over. Surely goodness and mercy shall follow me all the days of my life; and I will dwell in the house of the Lord forever." ***Psalms 23:1-6***

Everything David wrote here was in reference to his personal relationship with the Lord. All of the comparisons he used were taken from the role of a shepherd in relation to his sheep. According to information taken directly from ***Psalms 23:1-6*** we see the shepherd is responsible for:

➤ Leading the sheep to food and water.

➤ For maintaining a sense of preservation and order which keeps fear out.

Defining the Gifts

➤ For providing discipline and unity with the rod and staff.

In summary, the natural shepherd lived among one flock of sheep in order to provide constant care and supervision for that particular flock. This care and supervision could be categorized as: ***nourishment, protection, order, and discipline.*** Why does the owner of the flock need a shepherd? In other words, why does he want the sheep fed, protected, ordered, and disciplined? The answer is simple, but profound, and will have a dramatic impact on helping to define the office of pastor. The owner of the sheep is interested in having the sheep fed, protected, ordered, and disciplined so they will bear wool, produce off-spring in a constant cycle, and increase in numbers and quality. The shepherd feeds, protects, orders, and disciplines the sheep so that, as healthy sheep, they can produce increase for the owner of the sheep. This is the whole point for the owner of the sheep: ***I n c r e a s e !***

Shepherd as a Hebrew term was used in the Old Testament in much the same manner as in the New Testament: both to identify a keeper of sheep and to refer to a minister for God's people. David has provided us a wonderful illustration from the Old Testament of a keeper of sheep. How do the natural shepherd illustrations work to help us understand an office of ministry given by God for the people of God?

The Lord God told Moses that he *(Moses)* was going to be,

> "Now the Lord said to Moses; "Go up into the Mount Abarim, and see the land which I have given to the children of Israel. And when you have seen it, you also shall be gathered to your people, as Aaron your brother was gathered... Then Moses spoke to the Lord, saying:...

Temple of Glory

> *"...Let the Lord, the God of the spirits of all flesh, set a man over the congregation, who may go out before them and go in before them, who may lead them out and bring them in, that the congregation of the Lord may not be like sheep which have no shepherd."*
> *Numbers 27:12,13, 15-17*

Here Moses was equating his position as leader of Israel to one of shepherd to sheep. Moses' desire for the people of God was that after he *(Moses)* was taken from the people, they would not be left as sheep without a shepherd.

We must, however, be careful with this illustration seeing Moses as *"...the shepherd..."* over all Israel. It can lead us into a wrong understanding of the shepherd's role and responsibilities. Moses' leadership over all Israel was a type of Christ over all believers, and not typical for all shepherds. Jesus is the chief shepherd over the entire flock of God. Jesus describes this relationship He has with the church.

> *"...I am the good shepherd; and I know My sheep, and am known by My own. As the Father knows Me, even so I know the Father; and I lay down My life for the sheep. And other sheep (Gentiles) I have which are not of this fold (Jews); them also I must bring, and they will hear My voice; and there will be one flock and one shepherd..."* **John 10:14-16**

Jesus is the head of the Church and supreme authority over all its affairs. **There are no other positions of leadership with supreme authority within the Church on any level.** Any leader with any authority at all must be in submission to the will and authority of Jesus as the chief shepherd of the one true flock

Defining the Gifts

of God. Every function of any church on any level must be considered as parts of one sheepfold with Jesus as *"...the shepherd..."!*

God, Himself, spoke of shepherds as ministers to the people in several of the Old Testament books of the prophets. Three accounts in Ezekiel, Jeremiah, and Isaiah will help promote understanding of the use of the term *"...shepherd..."* as a minister to people.

> *"And the word of the Lord came to me, saying, "Son of man, prophesy against the shepherds of Israel, prophesy and say to them, 'Thus says the Lord God to the shepherds: Woe to the shepherds of Israel who feed themselves! Should not the shepherds feed the flocks?"*
> **Ezekiel 34:1,2**

In this scripture God is making it absolutely clear one of the responsibilities of the shepherd was to **"...feed the people...".**

> *"Go and proclaim these words toward the north, and say: Return, backsliding Israel, says the Lord; I will not cause My anger to fall on you. For I am merciful, says the Lord; I will not remain angry forever. Only acknowledge your iniquity, that you have transgressed against the Lord your God, and have scattered your charms to alien deities under every green tree, and you have not obeyed My voice, says the Lord. Return, O backsliding children, says the Lord; for I am married to you. I will take you, one from a city and two from a family, and I will bring you to Zion. And I will give you shepherds according to My heart, who will feed you with knowledge and understanding."* **Jeremiah 3:12-15**

The Lord is making it very specific what the shepherds are required to feed the people: **"...*knowledge and understanding*...".**

Temple of Glory

"O Zion, you who bring good tidings, get up into the high mountain; O Jerusalem, you who bring good tidings, lift up your voice with strength, lift it up, be not afraid; say to the cities of Judah, "Behold your God!" Behold, the Lord God shall come with a strong hand, and His arm shall rule for Him; Behold, His reward is with Him, and His work before Him. He will feed His flock like a shepherd; He will gather the lambs with His arm, and carry them in His bosom, and gently lead those who are with young." **Isaiah 40:9-11**

Jesus Himself illustrates the role of a shepherd revealing the various aspects of the function of *"...shepherd..."*: **Providing constant care and supervision in the areas of nourishment, protection, order and discipline.**

Just as we asked the question why does an owner of natural sheep want or need a shepherd, so, too, we ask why does God as owner of spiritual sheep want or need a shepherd? In other words, why does God want His flock fed, protected, ordered, and disciplined? The answers are much the same as for the natural shepherd. **God is interested in having His people increase.**

"...from whom the whole body, joined and knit together by what every joint supplies, according to the effective working by which every part does its share, causes growth of the body for the edifying of itself in love..."
Ephesians 4:16

Shepherds feed, protect, order, and discipline the sheep so they can grow in knowledge and understanding, in order to be able to prosper and increase in God.

It would be presumptuous to assume only one spiritual shepherd, or *"...pastor..."* as only one ministry gift given by

Defining the Gifts

Christ is individually responsible for providing all of the care and supervision required to nourish, protect, order, and discipline the sheep. Christ has given five gifts, apostles, prophets, evangelists, pastors, and teachers to produce perfected saints and a unified body,

> *"...till we all come to the unity of the faith and of the knowledge of the Son of God, to a perfect man, to the measure of the stature of the fullness of Christ; that we should no longer be children, tossed to and fro and carried about with every wind of doctrine, by the trickery of men, in the cunning craftiness of deceitful plotting, but, speaking the truth in love, may grow up in all things into Him who is the head, Christ, from whom the whole body, joined and knit together by what every joint supplies, according to the effective working by which every part does its share, causes growth of the body for the edifying of itself in love."* **Ephesians 13-16**

All five offices have a part to play in helping to meet the goal of producing perfected saints and a unified body!

PASTOR DEFINED

Then what is the function of the office of *"...pastor..."*? We can define, in-principle, the office of pastor as a local ministry. He provides constant care and supervision for a particular flock. He nourishes, protects, orders, and disciplines as we have seen exemplified in both the natural shepherd and the spiritual shepherd of the Old Testament. However, one ingredient must be added to our definition which has not been much of a consideration in the past. This ingredient is the *"...pastor..."* must participate with the offices of apostle, prophet, evangelist, and teacher to help produce perfected saints and a unified body in the flock.

Temple of Glory

We have already seen the apostle, prophet, evangelist, pastor, and teacher have all five been given responsibilities to help produce perfected saints and a unified body. Each office relates to Jesus from the perspective of their particular calling. They impart the knowledge they receive from their relationship with the Christ to the saints. Their ministries help the saints grow in relationship with God. Each of the five offices see only a part of what there is to see of Christ. All five are needed to present a complete revelation of Christ to the church. Without all five offices ministering to the church, the flock could not achieve the increase God has planned.

In order to maintain consistency in defining all of the offices of ministry we must see each of them from a building type of mind-set, including the office of pastor. If we view the office of pastor from a shepherd-sheep perspective only, we will lose sight of his role in the building process. The office of pastor is a builder just like the other four offices. Involvement of all five offices is required in the construction process to build the Temple of the Lord.

TEACHER

The non-Christian Greek usage of the term *"...didaskalos..."*, from which the English term *"...teacher..."* is translated, ranges in meaning from teacher, master of instruction, schoolmaster, chorus-master, to poet in application.

> "The "...didaskalos..." is not just a teacher in general, but a man who teaches definite skills like reading, fighting, or music, developing the

Defining the Gifts

aptitudes already present...The decisive point is that systematic instruction is given...". **Kittel Theological Dictionary,** Volume II, Page 149

In the New Testament the term is used fifty-eight times. Forty-one of those occurrences are within the gospels referring to Jesus and seven times referring to other persons. The generic New Testament meaning is instructor, master, or teacher.

The office of *"...teacher..."* is an individually unique office of ministry in its own right. Luke recorded,

> *"Now in the church that was at Antioch there were certain prophets and teachers..."* **Acts 13:1**

Paul wrote, God, Himself set some in the church,

> *"And God has appointed these in the church: first apostles, second prophets, third teachers..."*
> **I Corinthians 12:28**

Paul then asked,

> *"...are all apostles? are all prophets? are all teachers?..."* **I Corinthians 12:29**

These questions are rhetorical devices used to mean all are not apostles, all are not prophets, and all are not teachers. But certainly there are some who are apostles, prophets, and teachers.

Temple of Glory

There are many illustrations of teaching in the Scriptures. The letter to the Hebrew Christians, written to believers in general, implies that every believer is supposed to teach.

> *"For though by this time you ought to be teachers, you need someone to teach you again the first principles of the oracles of God; and you have come to need milk and not solid food."* **Hebrews 5:12**

The importance on the role of *"...teaching..."* can be seen throughout the scriptures.

> *"...Does not even nature itself teach you..."*
> **I Corinthians 12:28,29**

> *"...the anointing teaches you all things..."* **I John 2:27**

> *"...the Helper, the Holy Spirit, whom the Father will send in My name, He will teach you all things..."* **John 14:26**

> *"...as My Father taught Me, I speak these things..."*
> **John 8:28**

> *"Go therefore and make disciples of all the nations, baptizing them in the name of the Father and of the Son and of the Holy Spirit, teaching them to observe all things that I have commanded you..."* **Matthew 28:19,20**

In these few scripture references nature teaches, the anointing teaches, the Holy Spirit teaches, the Father teaches, and the disciples are to teach.

With so many illustrations of *"...teachers..."*, ranging from *"...nature..."* to *"...Holy Spirit..."*, how can we define the office of teacher as an office of ministry so it is uniquely

Defining the Gifts

identifiable, or is there a difference? Perhaps everyone who teaches can be identified as a *"...teacher..."* in the ministry. We can eliminate this possibility because we have already understood it is the calling of God that makes you who you are, not what you do, and in Paul's letter to the church at Corinth we have already seen,

> *"...God has appointed these in the church: first apostles, second prophets, third teachers... Are all apostles? Are all prophets? Are all teachers?..."*
> **I Corinthians 12:28,29**

Narrow definitions of the offices of ministry have caused us to view the function of the offices too narrowly, as well. The function of each office can be seen in a broader range of settings than merely from the pulpit standing before a group of people. Such a narrow view easily corrupts our understanding of the office of teacher. We must open our hearts to consider each office of ministry from the perspective of the One Who gave them.

While gathering the information required to define the office of *"...teacher..."* it is essential that we begin with the understandings...

➤ ...the office is an individually unique office called by God,

➤ ...given as a gift of ministry to the church, and

➤ ...not everyone is one.

Because we have also already understood that each office of ministry has specific responsibilities with the corresponding authority required to fulfill those responsibilities, so our definition will revolve around these two understandings.

It might seem obvious what the responsibilities of a *"...teacher..."* are. The pre-Christ Greek use of the term gives us significant help in expanding the definition of a *"...teacher..."*. **Kittel Theological Dictionary** says the teacher was,

> "...not just a teacher in general, but a man who teaches definite skills like reading, fighting, or music, developing the aptitudes already present...systematic instruction...".

Our understanding must not come entirely from pre-Christ Greek use of the term, or **Kittel Theological Dictionary**, but the Holy Spirit's inspiration to use the term allows us to draw at least basic understanding of the term from its Greek use, just as we have done with the other offices of ministry.

Paul wrote in his letter to the church at Corinth,

> *"According to the grace of God which was given to me, as a wise master builder I have laid the foundation, and another builds on it. But let each one take heed how he builds on it."* ***I Corinthians 3:10***

Defining the Gifts

In the same letter and in the same context Paul continued,

> *"Let a man so account of us, as of the ministers of Christ, and stewards of the mysteries of God."*
> **I Corinthians 4:1**

Ministers of Christ are to be stewards of the mysteries of God. The ministry gift who builds on the foundation laid by the apostles and the prophets must minister the mysteries of God as a steward. In other words, his responsibility is to minister according to the hearers' growth and need to help produce skills in the believers so they can go on to the next level of spiritual growth. This area of responsibility is similar for a natural builder who builds on the foundation laid by another. Such a builder adds construction to the building so the next stage in the process can be done.

Using a modified secular Greek definition we can begin to put the term *"...teacher..."* in proper perspective for use in the church:

> "The *"...teacher..."* is not just a teacher in general, but a person who teaches definite skills like faith, healing, or worship, building on the foundation already laid...systematic instruction is given...".

This modified statement about the teacher will help identify the responsibilities of the teacher as a gift of ministry. God who has given these responsibilities has equipped the teacher with corresponding authority necessary to produce these *"...skills..."* in the believers to whom he ministers.

TEACHER DEFINED

In principle then, the office of *"...teacher..."* can be defined as a ministry gift who systematically instructs the church in specific areas of need, building upon a previously laid foundation. His ministry is not just to inform through teaching but to teach to produce definite skills. In the secular education system too often teaching is a wasted effort because it merely passes on information which the student is not motivated to learn except to pass an examination.

The office of teacher as a ministry gift given to the church must be presented to the church as a *"...skills producer..."*, rather than as an *"...information giver..."*. This should cause a new rapport to develop between the teacher as a minister and the believers receiving his ministry. It will also place more importance of the aspect of *"...stewarding the mysteries..."* on the teacher's part. He will have to have a more intimate relationship with the believers to whom he ministers than merely teaching his favorite subjects from the Word. He will need to know more about those to whom he ministers to keep from just passing on information they are unmotivated to learn. His teaching must fit into the current flow of growth for the local assembly. The correct subject ministered at the correct time will cause the believers' spiritual growth to leap forward. This should make the teacher's ministry more acceptable and in greater demand. This concept will also help relieve the teacher from feeling he has to have some new deep revelation to please the congregation. Rather, the congregation will be eager to receive the teacher's ministry on faith, or healing, or worship, or whatever the next skill needed to move them onward in their spiritual growth.

Defining the Gifts

SUMMARY STATEMENT

The in-principle definitions have been given without providing a list of specific ministry responsibilities, authority, or equipment. Many facets of each office of ministry have not been considered in these brief sections. The in-principle definitions were intended to help expand the view of each office so the Holy Spirit can begin to reveal to us what we have been missing from each office by defining them too narrowly. For example, the apostle as a *"...foundation layer..."* gives us a greater opportunity to benefit from the office than apostle as *"...church starter..."*. The evangelist as a *"...material gather...,"* presenting Jesus as Savior to the lost *and* to the saints opens a new dimension for the office to the church.

Too narrowly defining each office of ministry with our understanding closed to realizing there is anything more than our narrow definition, tends to make us err. For example, believing an evangelist is not a true New Testament evangelist unless he has signs and miracles following his ministry. Every believer is expected to do the works of Jesus. If a believer does not cast out devils, lay hands on the sick, and speak with authority, does that mean he is not a true New Testament believer? If so, there are numerous people in the church on the earth today who are not true New Testament believers. Of course a person can be a believer even though he has not cast out a devil or laid hands on the sick! Casting out devils and laying hands on the sick to see the sick recover are by-products of being a believer, not qualifications to define whether you are a believer. This type of thinking will most definitely lead people into error. It is the call of God which makes a person an evangelist, not signs and miracles. It is faith in God that makes a person a believer, not doing the works of Jesus. Receiving each office of ministry according to these in-principle definitions and seeing their ministries function accordingly in the church will cause us to grow in understanding of each office. Moving one step at a time to expand our understanding of the apostle, prophet, evangelist, pastor, and teacher will open the door for God to give us the increase. God will give us understanding in revelation, understanding, and relationship. Our responsibility is to hunger to grow in each of these areas.

Chapter Eight

INTERRELATIONSHIPS BETWEEN MINISTRY GIFTS

It is without question that God has set the gifts of ministry in the church. All five of the offices of ministry have been given by Christ Jesus as gifts to the entire church. The question which is not satisfactorily answered is: *"Are these five offices of apostle, prophet, evangelist, pastor, and teacher supposed to interact in any way?"* Or are they each only responsible for their individual tasks without any type of interrelationship? In order to see the gifts function in the church as God intended, we must answer these questions according to the Word.

GOAL OF MINISTRY

Establishing the goal for all five offices collectively will help our understanding regarding interrelationships. The apostle Paul wrote the five offices have been given,

> *"For the equipping of the saints, for the work of the ministry, for the edifying of the body of Christ, till we all come to the unity of the faith and of the knowledge of the Son of God, to a perfect man, to the measure of the stature of the fullness of Christ..."* **Ephesians 4:12,13**

Even though there are five different offices of ministry, there is really only one goal: **"...*a perfect man...*"**.

Temple of Glory

This goal can be stated another way. We have already gained understanding regarding the commission of the Christ and His body; it is to build one Temple of the Lord. This temple is composed of living stones who are born again believers. We also know from Paul's letter to the saints at Ephesus,

> *"...we are members of His body, of His flesh and of His bones..."* **Ephesians 5:30**

The flesh and bone body of Christ is also composed of born again believers. The Temple of the Lord and the Body of Christ are just different terms for the same thing. Producing a perfect man and building the Temple of the Lord is the same goal. The goal of all five offices of ministry is to build the Temple of the Lord into a perfect man.

The most productive mind-set we could adopt regarding the five offices of ministry apostle, prophet, evangelist, pastor, and teacher would be a building mind-set. For a natural building to be completed each builder must interact with the other builders. A natural building is constructed in stages with each new stage built on a previously completed stage. The foundational stage is the first, not necessarily in order of importance, but in building order. It is impossible to construct the roof without sidewalls being constructed first. The roofers and sidewall builders wait until they have a proper foundation on which to build. Even when the foundation is being laid, other building jobs are being done in cooperation with the laying of the foundation. For example, some of the plumbing must be put in place before the entire foundation can be completed. It would not only be virtually impossible,

Interrelationships

but also incredibly more costly for any builder to enter a construction site and endeavor to do his particular job from start to finish without interacting with the other builders involved in the building project. Some type of communication between builders is simply required for the builders to work in a cooperative manner to produce the completed goal.

We are all involved in a building project in the church, building the Temple of the Lord. Paul used such building terminology in writing to the Corinthians. He wrote,

> *"For we are God's fellow workers; you are God's field, you are God's building. According to the grace of God which was given to me, as a wise master builder I have laid the foundation, and another builds on it. But let each one take heed how he builds on it."*
> **I Corinthians 3:9,10**

In order for the building project of the church to be completed, each of the ministry gifts as builders must interact with the other ministry gifts as builders.

DOMAIN OF MINISTRY

Before we can examine the level of interrelationship between the five offices of ministry as builders, it is necessary to determine where their ministries function. In other words, what is the domain of ministry of each of the five offices? The church's current understanding says the pastor is set in a local church, and the apostle, prophet, evangelist, and teacher are all set in the church universal as traveling ministries. But are there really two domains of ministry operating within the church on the earth? Perhaps we need a definition of the term

Temple of Glory

"...church..." before we can consider the domain of ministry gifts. The English term *"...church..."* is used as a translation for the Greek term *"...ekkleesia..."*. This Greek term was not unique to the Christian church; it was used before Jesus came onto the earth. The secular use of the term was defined as *"...called out ones..."* and used for public gatherings. Therefore, we simply cannot rely on the Greek definition or use to give us accurate revelation defining the Christian church.

We can apply the meaning of the pre-Christ Greek definition for *"...ekkleesia..."* as *"...called out ones..."* to every Christian as a starting place to define *"...church..."*. The apostles, Peter and Paul, both wrote about what happens when a person is born again.

> *"...you are a chosen generation, a royal priesthood, a holy nation, His own special people, that you may proclaim the praises of Him Who called you out of darkness into His marvelous light; who once were not a people but are now the people of God, who had not obtained mercy but now have obtained mercy."*
> **I Peter 2:9,10**

> *"He (God) has delivered us from the power of darkness and conveyed us into the kingdom of the Son of His love."*
> **Colossians 1:13**

When a person is born again he is *"...called out..."* of darkness into the marvelous light of God. In this *"...called out..."* sense the pre-Christ Greek definition easily applies to every Christian. This application applies to all believers everywhere on the earth and those who have already gone on to heaven. For the purpose of this writing only those believers who re-

Interrelationships

main on the earth are to be considered. The application of the term to all believers everywhere makes that group the universal *"...ekkleesia..."* or the church universal.

The *"...ekkleesia..."* of Christian believers have a very intimate status. The Holy Spirit inspired Paul to refer to that group as,

> *"...members of His (Jesus') body, of His flesh, and of His bones..."* **Ephesians 5:30**

The Holy Spirit also inspired Paul to write to the church at Corinth,

> *"...by one Spirit we were all baptized into one body, whether Jews or Greeks, whether slaves or free, and have all been made to drink into one Spirit..."*
> **I Corinthians 12:13**

Because Christians are the flesh and bone body of Christ Jesus, we understand how there can only be one body of Christ, but is there only one church?

The term *"...body..."* in relation to the body of Christ has been very loosely used. The term has been very commonly used to refer to believers who comprise a single local assembly. This usage has very commonly been extended to mean all of the individual bodies of local assemblies when viewed collectively comprising the body of Christ. This application of the term *"...body..."* can be used to refer to students in a local school setting or perhaps other groups of people. However, we cannot accurately do so in the spiritual sense regarding the body of Christ. Every local assembly is a *"...body..."* of people in the *"...student body..."* sense, but not in the spiritual sense. There are not many bodies of Christ on the earth; there is only one, made up of many members.

We cannot in any sense say
there are many bodies of Christ on the earth!

However, the term *"...ekkleesia..."* translated *"...church..."* is different. Anytime two or more persons who are *"...called out..."* to meet in Jesus' name can be referred to as an *"...ekkleesia..."* in the same way people in Ephesus who were *"...called out..."* for a secular meeting to consider the subject of the goddess Diana were referred to as an *"...ekkleesia..." (see **Acts 19:21-41**)*. In this sense, with two or more people gathered together in Jesus' name, there are in fact many *"...ekkleesia..."* or *"...churches..."* on the earth. These many churches together comprise the body of Christ collectively and, of course, with those believers who have already gone to heaven.

If the term *"...ekkleesia..."* is used in the extended sense to refer to the worldwide group of all Christians everywhere on the earth, we can easily see how there is one church on the earth to which we refer to as the church universal. However, the church universal in this sense is unworkable as an entity to describe the domain of ministry in which the saints are to be perfected. The work of the ministry of the five offices of ministry is not taking place in the church universal as a collective group. No one could minister to such a group, as a group, except our omnipotent and omnipresent God. Rather, this

Interrelationships

universal church is composed of many local churches which can be broken down for convenient reference into smaller groups. An example would be, by continent referring to the church of North America, the church of Africa, and so on. We can break these classifications down even further by state, city, and finally individually identifiable groups.

There may be special corporate church meetings held within nations, states, or cities, but consistent regular ministry in which the saints are to be perfected takes place within the individually identifiable groups. These groups are referred to as *"...local assemblies..."*.

Perhaps a natural illustration will make it clearer. There is a nationwide group of individuals in the U.S.A. who are all members of one organization. This organization is called the National Football League (N.F.L.). The N.F.L. is composed of individually identifiable groups referred to as teams. Each team is composed of individual players. The goal of each team is to produce perfected players so the team can achieve success and thereby prosper.

The domain where all the work takes place to perfect the players is in each team, not in the N.F.L. Certainly, each team is a part of the N.F.L., but the N.F.L. is simply a term used to identify the whole network of teams and players. Strategies, rewards, discipline, goals and the like are primarily oriented to each specific team, not to the N.F.L. as such. Of course the N.F.L. has overall strategies, rewards, discipline, and goals for the whole league, but practical application of these takes place primarily within each individual team. Any illustration will break down at some point, however, this illustration is given merely to help us develop an understanding of the practical domain for the church on the earth.

The church universal as a group is not the domain of ministry for the five offices of ministry. There are not two domains of ministry where the five office of ministry operate within the church to perfect the saints. There may be corporate meetings conducted where many churches come together for special ministry, but the personal, consistent, and regular ministry for the purpose of perfecting the saints takes place within the local church. Christ gave five offices for the perfecting of the saints. If these five offices are going to help perfect the saints, they must minister to them on a consistent regular basis. We can say, then, the primary domain of ministry for the apostle, prophet, evangelist, pastor, and teacher ministering to the saints in order to help perfect them is the local church.

OFFICES IN MANIFESTATION

Just because the primary domain of ministry to perfect the saints is the local assembly does not require all five offices of ministry to be resident on staff in every local church. The conclusion is simple: Even if the apostle, prophet, evangelist, and teacher were trans-local ministries, the domain in which they help perfect the saints cannot be a universal domain. That domain does not exist as a domain in which saints can be perfected. Saints are resident in an individual

Interrelationships

local assembly and require ministry focused on helping perfect them in that environment. A natural world illustration of a builder will add to our understanding in this matter.

An electrician may own his own business and sub-contract out to various general contractors. The electrician cannot ply his trade in a universal sense; he must work on an individual sense. That is, he must have specific contracts to do specific electrical tasks on specific building projects. This illustration can be leveraged over into the spiritual world and applied to the five offices of ministry. Apostles, prophets, evangelists, and teachers may have their own ministries and move about to minister in various local assemblies. The offices of ministry cannot ply their trade in a universal sense *(except as we have already made mention, in special corporate meetings involving various local assemblies)*, they must work on an individual sense. That is they must have specific invitations to do specific ministry tasks in specific local assemblies.

Jesus' intent in giving five different offices of ministry was for them to provide five different ministries. If the ministry of the apostle and the evangelist was designed to be the same, they could have been called by the same name. However, Jesus gave two different gifts two different names because they were not designed to be the same. In science students are taught the benefit of considering subject matter in regards to how the matter is alike and how it is different. Both considerations have benefits to the scientist. We understand how the five offices of ministry are alike; we also need to understand how they are different. They are alike in that they all help produce perfected saints and a unified body. They are different in that they all have specific and different functions from one another. They are alike in that they all minister revelation of Christ to the saints. They are different in that they all minister a different revelation of Christ to the saints. They are alike in that God has given them authority and equipment necessary to fulfill their ministry responsibilities. They are different in that each of their authority and equipment is different from the others'.

The supernatural manifestation of the authority and equipment of each of the offices of ministry individually, working collectively with all of the other individual offices of ministry, will produce perfected saints and a unified body. Understanding the responsibilities, authority, and equipment of the offices, and the domain of ministry in which their roles are to become practical will open the door for their roles to produce the increase for which we are looking.

NO CORPORATE OFFICES

The understanding in which the contemporary church has operated is that four of the five offices of ministry are set in the church universal and only one is set in the church local. This understanding practically but efficiently stops the authority and equipment of four of the five offices from working on behalf of the saints. The offices of ministry have been given to perfect the saints, and the saints are perfected in the local environment, not the universal environment. If we can take

Interrelationships

this one simple step and change the mind-set regarding the domain of ministry for the offices of ministry, then we will take a huge leap forward in seeing the Lord's design work in the church on the earth.

We have created an artificial corporate-type separation between the church universal and the church local. This type of separation exists in large corporations in the natural world. A large corporation may have many local offices through which its primary business is conducted. The majority of the employees function within these local offices of business. A limited percentage of the corporation's employees actually staff the corporate office. Corporate offices are generally considered to be a higher hierarchical level than local offices. Terminology from the corporate staff is oriented to corporate goals, requirements, and the like. The corporation takes on an identity as if it were a real person. Corporate and local offices are distinctly separate.

There is no such separation within the body of Christ. We are to function as a body with each part functioning according to calling in order to help bring life to the whole body. All five offices of ministry have been set in the body with the same overall goal: produce one perfect man *("...Build the temple of the Lord, in other terms...")*. All five offices of ministry are part of the universal church, and all five minister to believers who are parts of the universal church. However, these believers as parts of the universal church receive ministry to be perfected in identifiable groups known as the local church. There are no corporate offices where the apostle, prophet, evangelist, and teacher are headquartered known as the universal church. There is no one group known as the church universal to whom these four offices minister as corporate staff on a higher level than the local church. Rather, these four offices minister to Christians in individually identifiable groups known as local churches. Local churches are made up of Christians who are the body of Christ.

> *(NOTE: We understand the evangelist has as his primary ministry gathering stones, but we also know he, too, has responsibility to minister to the saints to help perfect them. It is his ministry to the saints to which we are referring here that takes place in the local church.)*

LEADERSHIP IN THE CHURCH

The apostle Peter admonished the elders to,

> *"Shepherd the flock of God which is among you, serving as overseers, not by compulsion but willingly, not for dishonest gain but eagerly; not as being lords over those entrusted to you, but being examples to the flock;"*
> *I Peter 5:2,3*

The whole concept of *"...in charge..."* or *"...in control..."* of the local church is corrupt. The local church has become an entity on its own without the people. However, the church does not exist on any level without the people. The church is people! Believers are the church on the earth. Rather than clashing over who is in charge of an entity that does not exist without people, we need to see what exactly we have been placed within the church to do. **The offices of ministry are gifts to the church. The church is not a gift to the offices of ministry.** The offices of ministry have been given as gifts to the church to provide the believers the necessary revelation to grow in grace to a perfect man and become unified as the body of Christ.

Interrelationships

Rather than being controlled by a corrupt concept of who is in charge, we must instead re-establish the true purpose of the offices of ministry and work together to fulfill our purpose as gifts to the church. Imagine all five offices of ministry seeing clearly these simple truths:

➤ *Jesus, and Jesus alone, is the Head of the Church at every level!*

➤ *We have been given by Christ to the church.*

➤ *Our purpose is to provide living revelation of Christ necessary for the church to grow in grace.*

➤ *Our goal is to produce perfected saints and a unified body.*

➤ *We are all builders required to work together to build the Temple of the Lord.*

➤ *We are to be examples to the flock.*

Leadership can be provided basically two ways: control or motivation. A tyrant leads by control. People usually follow the tyrant out of fear. A ministry gift of God leads through motivation. People follow because of the example of the minister's own supernatural life. A called minister of God has divinely given authority that no man can take from him. It takes the wisdom of God to exercise the authority of God in order to provide a supernatural example for the people to desire to follow.

If a minister knows his calling and the authority that accompanies it, two things will happen:

1. He will be secure in God to exercise his authority from God to lead by motivation, not by control.

2. He will recognize the limitations of his authority and reach out to other gifted and called ministry gifts with authority and equipment to help lead.

No one office of ministry is equipped to do it all! It takes the apostle, the prophet, the evangelist, the pastor, and the teacher all working within the scope of their calling and authority to provide the leadership necessary to perfect the saints.

Each office provides leadership within the church by the example he sets according to his calling. Each office recognizes the limitation of his own authority and hungers to walk together with the other offices of ministry to be able to provide the comprehensive leadership necessary to lead the saints into perfection and unity.

Most of the controversy of *"...control..."* of the local church is outside the scope of perfecting the saints and more in the realm of natural administration and finances. However, control of the local church is not our goal. ***The local church is people and our goal is not to control people.*** Our goal is to help produce a perfect man. The apostles set a standard for supernatural ministry to achieve this goal in the early church for all five-fold ministry gifts.

"Now in those days, when the number of the disciples was multiplying, there arose a complaint against the Hebrews by the Hellenists, because their widows were

Interrelationships

neglected in the daily distribution. Then the twelve summoned the multitude of the disciples and said, It is not desirable that we should leave the word of God and serve tables. Therefore, brethren, seek out from among you seven men of good reputation, full of the Holy Spirit and wisdom, whom we may appoint over this business; but we will give ourselves continually to prayer and to the ministry of the word. " **Acts 6:1-4**

The main interest of the five offices of ministry today should be only one thing:

How do we see the saints perfected and unified so the Temple of the Lord can be built!

When we realize no one office can perfect the saints, but rather it takes all five ministering consistently and regularly to the saints to perfect them, then we will begin to see the value of interrelationship between the gifts of ministry.

INTERRELATIONSHIP BETWEEN MINISTRY GIFTS

Now, what exactly is the interrelationship between ministry gifts within the church? In order to begin to answer this question we must restate that all five offices of ministry form a ministry unit given by Christ for producing perfected saints and a unified body *("...building the Temple of the Lord...")*. They are like spokes of a wheel, each one is necessary to get the job done.

The evangelist goes into the field to gather materials for the building project. After he has *"...hewed..."* them out of the mountain of darkness, he does not merely leave them alone and strewn individually all over the landscape. Rather, he helps them as new living stones and building materials to find the construction site to be added to the Temple of the Lord.

These new living stones are *babes-in-Christ*, and cannot effectively choose where they should go to be fed the sincere milk of the Word any more than a natural babe can find an appropriate parent. They are ignorant of the ways of the kingdom of God and of their own spiritual needs. The evangelist is their first contact with a leader in the body of Christ after being born again. He is the most natural choice to help move them in the right direction to begin their spiritual development. Obviously, the evangelist must interact with the other ministry gifts regarding the new living stones coming to the construction site. Each time he leads people to Christ this process will be repeated.

SPIRITUAL EDUCATION

Upon arrival at the construction site construction begins on the new living stones. They must be built as individual temples of the Lord and shown how to fit into the corporate Temple of the Lord. The Holy Spirit baptized each one into Christ, but each new believer needs to know how to take his place in-Christ in the local assembly. All five offices of ministry will be needed to help fulfill these two goals at some point in the new believer's spiritual journey.

The saints cannot effectively be perfected by ministering to them corporately primarily because they represent mul-

Interrelationships

tiple levels of spiritual maturity. Even in the natural world the academic community determined years ago how ineffective the education process was when gathering multiple levels of students together in a single environment. The days of little red school houses full of students ranging from elementary school through high school are a thing of the past. Gathering the saints together corporately for the purpose of ministering revelation of Christ to them for their spiritual growth cannot be done with any degree of stewardship or success. A corporate gathering for exhortation, comfort, encouragement, praise & worship, ordination, partaking of holy ordinances, and the like are all the will of God and very profitable. The saints need corporate gatherings for all levels of spiritual growth, just not for the purpose of ministering revelation of Christ for their spiritual growth.

Typically, the local church meets three times per week in which an average time of one hour each service is allotted to the ministry of the Word. In the natural world our children attend school approximately six and one half hours per day. Even a very conservative estimate of actual classroom instruction would be more than the amount of ministry of the Word for the church in an entire week. A typical school system has approximately 175 taught days in the public schools in a school year *(nine month school year)*. With a conservative estimate of five hours of classroom instruction per school day, that amounts to 875 hours of instruction per school year. Comparing the typical local church's three hours per week times fifty-two weeks a year, it would take the local church over five and one half years to provide the same amount of instruction in the Word as our children receive class room instruction in nine months. It would take over sixty-six years to provide equivalent instruction as twelve years of public school.

Of course this is not an exact parallel to compare educating the soul with educating the spirit. Students in school grow in quantity and understanding of information. The believers in-Christ grow in quality of relationship with the Word as a living person. However, we can easily see if we expect to perfect babes-in-Christ so they can mature in-Christ, we are going to have to spend more quality time with them than three corporate hours per week.

We send our children to school for a minimum of twelve school years. Why do we spend so much time, money, and effort to educate our children? We do so because we know they must be educated in order to survive in our sophisticated world. Educators have determined it takes a minimum of twelve school years to accomplish that goal. How much more should we recognize the necessity of educating Christians in the realm of the spirit. The prophet Hosea received a word from the Lord saying,

> "*My people are destroyed because of a lack of knowledge...*" **Hosea 4:6**

To how many Christians does this word apply today? People come into the kingdom as newborn babes with need to develop skills to combat principalities, powers, rulers of darkness of this world, and spiritual wickedness in high places. How many Christians are skilled in the use of their weapons because of their training? How many even know who the enemy is or what his devices are?

Interrelationships

RE-EVALUATING OUR METHODS

There is a great need to spend more time with the believers to help educate them in the spirit. Remember this education is not simply passing on information, but rather helping believers develop skills and a relationship with the Word as a person. However, whether it is passing on information or helping to develop skills and a relationship with Jesus, it is difficult to get commitment for three services per week already. How can we possibly consider restructuring our schedules to add more time to instruct the saints?

Perhaps it is not so much a restructuring of our time schedules as it is restructuring our methods. Individually exclusive environments for each level of spiritual growth are almost certainly going to be required in order for us to be effective. This type of stewardship is written about in the New Testament.

> "Let a man so consider us, as servants of Christ and stewards of the mysteries of God." *I Corinthians 4:1*

> "For though by this time you ought to be teachers, you need someone to teach you again the first principles of the oracles of God; and you have come to need milk and not solid food. For everyone who partakes only of milk is unskilled in the word of righteousness, for he is a babe. But solid food belongs to those who are of full age (mature), that is, those who by reason of use have their senses exercised to discern both good and evil."
> *Hebrews 5:12-14*

The clear orientation in the **Hebrews 5:12-14** reference is *"...skills..."* production. In order for one person to bring another person to a place of ability to perform a skill there must be more than just the passing on of information. There must be...

...*instruction,*

...*demonstration, and*

...*involvement.*

To minister the mysteries of God to the saints, milk to babes, and meat to the mature, in order to produce skills in them, we must have the saints in individually exclusive environments. It is impossible to expect our training to be successful if we try to minister to the new born and mature all in one hour, all in one environment. This is not good stewardship of the mysteries of God to the saints.

Chapter Nine

MINISTRY RELATIONSHIP WITH THE SAINTS

Paul writes about the responsibilities of the five offices of ministry,

> *"And He Himself (Jesus) gave some to be apostles, some prophets, some evangelist, and some pastors and teachers, for the equipping of the saints, for the work of ministry, for the edifying of the body of Christ..."*
> **Ephesians 4:11,12**

What about the saints? What are the ministry responsibilities of the saints?

Is the perfection of the saints a means unto an end: So they can do the work of the ministry in order for the church to grow? We do desire for the church to grow, but are we perfecting the saints in order to *"...use..."* them to achieve our corporate goals? We have already gained an understanding regarding God's purpose for redeeming man. Was part of God's purpose for our redemption to use us to be His servants?

SERVITUDE versus SONSHIP

Paul told the Corinthians their bodies were the temple of the Holy Ghost and that they were not their own.

Temple of Glory

> *"For you were bought at a price; therefore glorify God in your body and in your spirit, which are God's."*
> *I Corinthians 6:20*

It is without question that every believer is *"...bought and paid for..."* by God. However, look at the price God paid.

> *"...knowing that you were not redeemed with corruptible things, like silver or gold, from your aimless conduct received by tradition from your fathers, but with the precious blood of Christ, as of a lamb without blemish and without spot. He indeed was foreordained before the foundation of the world, but was manifest in these last times for you..."* ***I Peter 1:18-20***

The blood of God's very own Son is a pretty high price to pay just so God could staff His house with servants!

Paul writes to the church at Galatia regarding God's motive for paying such a high price for us.

> *"But when the fullness of the time had come, God sent forth His Son, born of a woman, born under the law, to redeem those who were under the law, that we might receive the adoption of sons. And because you are sons, God has sent forth the Spirit of His Son into your hearts, crying out, Abba, Father!"* ***Galatians 4:4-7***

God did not redeem us to be His servants. He redeemed us to be His sons. Sonship and Fatherhood are both individually focused. Sons are born one at a time, even in multiple birth deliveries. Each and every son is important. God loved the *"...whole world..."* so much He sent Jesus into the world to redeem us to make us His sons.

Relationship with Saints

> *"For God so loved the world that He gave His only begotten Son, that whoever believes in Him should not perish but have everlasting life."* **John 3:16**

Jesus' death provided salvation for the whole world, but that salvation works one person at a time.

God does not want the offices of ministry given by Christ to hurry up and perfect the saints so He can use them. The ministry gifts perfect the saints so they can walk supernaturally successful in relationship with the Father as His sons. Perfected saints as functional parts of the body will cause the church to grow but as a by-product of their growth in relationship with their God. Our primary focus must not be on corporate church growth but rather on perfecting the sons of God. Perfected saints will produce corporate church growth.

The offices of ministry help individual believers grow by ministering revelation of Christ to the saints. This revelation brings the believers into contact with knowledge about Jesus, but this knowledge about Jesus must undergo transformation to become relationship with Jesus. Increase in transformed knowledge of God the Father and of Jesus cause the believer to increase in quality of life to the kind of life like God Himself has. Jesus said,

> *"And this is eternal life, that they may know You, the only true God, and Jesus Christ whom You have sent."*
> **John 17:3**

Even though every new believer comes into Christ complete in Christ, every believer must grow in their knowledge of Christ.

Temple of Glory

There is a wonderful scriptural understanding for this.

> *"Now I say that the heir, as long as he is a child, does not differ at all from a slave, though he is master of all..."* **Galatians 4:1**

Ministry gift responsibility to help produce perfected saints is not so God can use them as servants, but so the believers can function as sons of God through relationship with God. Desire to minister to others and the ability to do so come out of our intimate relationship with God. Our God desires to reveal Himself to us as His sons so we can have the type of life that He Himself has. When our life becomes the same type that our Father has, we will look for ways to present that life to others.

John recorded Jesus as speaking to His disciples about the subject matter of *"...servants..."*.

> *"No longer do I call you servants, for a servant does not know what his master is doing; but I have called you friends, for all things that I heard from My Father I have made known to you."* **John 15:15**

The Father gave us His own Spirit to dwell in us in order to reveal to us the things He has prepared for us who love Him. According to Jesus this kind of information is not available to servants. Rather, we can see it is for sons.

> *"And because you are sons, God has sent forth the Spirit of His Son into your hearts, crying out, Abba, Father?"*
> **Galatians 4:6**

Relationship with Saints

Abba has redeemed us to be His sons and to function as His sons because we have a desire to do so, not because He owns us, and we have to do so. Jesus gave us the perfect example of the kind of relationship the Father desires. Jesus said,

> *"For I have come down from heaven, not to do My own will, but the will of Him who sent Me. This is the will of the Father who sent Me, that of all He has given Me I should lose nothing, but should raise it up at the last day. And this is the will of Him who sent Me, that everyone who sees the Son and believes in Him may have everlasting life; and I will raise him up at the last day."*
> **John 6:38-40**

Jesus, even though He was the Son of God, was submitted to do His Father's will as a loving Son. As God, Jesus did not have to do His Father's will. As God, Jesus chose to do His Father's will because He was perfectly in agreement with His Father. Two cannot walk together unless they are in agreement. The Father's will was motivated by His love for mankind. Jesus' will was motivated by His love for His Father and for mankind. This is a marvelous picture of God's great love.

INDIVIDUAL versus CORPORATE

Jesus gave us another illustration of His great love for us. He said of Himself,

> *"I am the good shepherd. The good shepherd gives His life for the sheep. But a hireling, he who is not the shepherd, one who does not own the sheep, sees the wolf coming and leaves the sheep and flees; and the wolf catches the sheep and scatters them."* **John 10:11-13**

Temple of Glory

While this portion of scripture is specifically about the good shepherd, it identifies an attitude that can be applied to each member of the body of Christ. If our focus is on perfecting the saints so they can fulfill the church's corporate goal, then we will produce servant attitudes in the saints causing the saints to live in a relationship with their Father out of a sense of duty like the hireling. If we focus on perfecting the saints so they can live like Jesus lived, then we will produce attitudes of service out of a relationship of love like the good shepherd. Both will cause the church to grow, but the servant mentality with the corporate goal in focus will not produce a perfect man edified in love. In order for the church to grow as Christ intended, the focus must be on perfecting individuals to be sons. Our God has designed everything about the church to revolve around His will for us to be sons. Christ's gifts of ministry were given to help move us forward in this concept.

> *"And He Himself gave some to be apostles, some prophets, some evangelists, and some pastors and teachers, for the equipping of the saints, for the work or ministry, for the edifying of the body of Christ, till we all come to the unity of the faith and of the knowledge of the Son of God, to a perfect men, to the measure of the stature of the fullness of Christ; that we should no longer be children, tossed to and fro and carried about with every wind of doctrine, by the trickery of men, in the cunning craftiness of deceitful plotting, but speaking the truth in love, may grow up in all things into Him who is the head, Christ, from whom the whole body, joined and knit together by what every joint supplies, according to the effective working by which every part does its share, causes growth of the body for the edifying of itself in love."*
> **Ephesians 4:11-16**

Relationship with Saints

One thing must become absolutely clear, the relationships of the offices of ministry with the saints, and the saints with other saints, must follow the pattern of scriptural models.

> *"And they continued steadfastly in the apostles' doctrine and fellowship, in the breaking of bread, and in prayers. Then fear came upon every soul, and many wonders and signs were done through the apostles. Now all who believed were together, and had all things in common, and sold their possessions and goods, and divided them among all, as anyone had need. So continuing daily with one accord in the temple, and breaking bread from house to house, they ate their food with gladness and simplicity of heart, praising God and having favor with all the people. And the Lord added to the church daily those who were being saved."* **Acts 2:42-47**

This passage of scripture is not meant to direct the body of Christ into communal living. Rather, it demonstrates the type of Christ-like relationships we are to have with one another: Relationships of unity motivated by love. Every member of the body has a part to play in order for the body to function as a body. Each member of the body must be individually identified and valued in order for that individual part to do what God expects them to do in the body. A functionally whole body fitly joined together requires relationships which unite the members to function as a unit, every joint supplying, according to the effective working by which every part does its share.

CHURCH-AS-A-BODY

Luke recorded in Acts,

> *"As they ministered to the Lord and fasted, the Holy Spirit said, "Now separate to Me Barnabas and Saul for the work to which I have called them."* **Acts 13:2**

These ministers were not being separated from the body of Christ, they were being separated unto a certain work within the body of Christ. This work was in relation to their calling to be apostles. They were set apart from other members of the church in the sense that *"...all are not apostles..."*. Their separation was for identification purposes so they could more effectively function as the parts of the body to which God had called them. The church needed to see that Paul and Barnabas were apostles in order for the church to be able to relate to them as such. This principle applies to every single member of the church. Jesus elaborated on this principle during one particular time of ministry to his disciples.

> *"...He who receives a righteous man in the name of a righteous man shall receive a righteous man's reward..."*
> **Matthew 10:41**

Every born again believer, the instant he is born again, becomes a son who enters into a parent-child relationship with God as Father. Abba's spiritual sons need to be parented in order to grow properly. Because God is the true parent of all of His spiritual sons, can anyone but God effectively parent believers as His children?

Relationship with Saints

SPIRITUAL PARENTING

The apostle Paul wrote of such matters in his letter to the saints at Corinth. He wrote,

> "...as my beloved children I warn you. For though you might have ten thousand instructors in Christ, yet you do not have many fathers; for in Christ Jesus I have begotten you through the gospel..."
> **I Corinthians 4:14-16**

In the spirit Paul was identifying himself as father, and the saints he referred to as his sons. The role-relationship Paul was defining here between himself and the saints was that of parent to child. Because God is the only true Father of the saints in the spirit, Paul's parental model must have some other meaning. What type of parent-child relationship did Paul have with the saints and why did he have such a relationship?

Paul makes it clear in his writings the goal of his work in ministry was to,

> "...present every man perfect in Christ Jesus..." **Colossians 1:28**

Also, as a five-fold ministry gift, we know he is partially responsible,

> "...for the equipping of the saints..." **Ephesians 4:12**

In other words, Paul was commissioned in part to see the saints grow up spiritually. This responsibility for natural parents is called *"...parenting..."*. As a minister called by God, then, Paul had a parental role with the saints to help them grow up spiritually. The kingdom of God is oriented to such family relationships. The parent-child model is in a constant evolutionary cycle. Even though God is the only true parent for all Christians, He has ordained parent-child relationships between saints as part of His plan to cause His children to receive effective parenting.

There are similar illustrations in the natural world to help our understanding in this parenting model. A child may lose his natural parents due to some catastrophe and need another natural family setting in which to live and grow. Such a child can be adopted by parents other than his true natural biological parents and parented effectively by his adoptive parents. In many nations of the world extended family members such as aunts, uncles, or grand-parents are often directly involved in the general process of parenting children within their families. In most third world environments older siblings within one family unit have specific parental responsibilities to help take care of their younger brothers and sisters. This parental role is generally very extensive to the point of providing the majority of the supervision and care for their little brothers and sisters including discipline and training.

MINISTRY RELATIONSHIPS

Using the family concept of the body of Christ we understand the growth process begins for all who are newly born again as babes-in-Christ. Because we have been given such terminology as babe to represent a person who is newly born

Relationship with Saints

again, we can easily conclude that other natural growth terms apply. A babe grows into a little child, who grows into a young man, who grows into an adult. These terms are all applicable to the maturation process of both natural children and spiritual children.

As a believer grows in-Christ through all of the stages of growth that lead him to become a mature believer, in each new level of growth he will have new responsibilities added to him, just like in a natural family. In-transit toward maturity each believer is expected to *"...freely give..."* what they have *"...freely received..."*. As each new believer is helped to develop relationship with Abba, with Jesus, and with the Holy Spirit they will also be helped to translate their newly acquired relationships into skills with which to live. They are expected in-turn to help others who have not yet had anyone help them. The writer of the letter to the Hebrews wrote these words,

> *"For though by this time you ought to be teachers, you need someone to teach you again the first principles of the oracles of God; and you have come to need milk and not solid food. For everyone who partakes only of milk is unskilled in the word of righteousness, for he is a babe. But solid food belongs to those who are of full age (mature), that is, those who by reason of use have their senses exercised to discern both good and evil."*
> **Hebrews 5:12,13**

The Holy Spirit has made it perfectly clear through the apostle Paul that although some have been given to be teachers, all have not been given to be teachers *(See **I Corinthians 12:28,29**)*. The writer of the letter to the Hebrews is not in conflict with Paul's writings. He is adding a new dimension of understanding to the revelation that came through Paul, that although all are not called to the office of teacher, all are expected to teach. This believer teaching believer is much like the sibling helping sibling concept we have already considered. As the church grows and every single believer needs personal hands-on help with his spiritual growth, God's means to meet these needs is for believers to help fellow believers.

Chapter Ten

PARENT-CHILD RELATIONSHIP MODEL

The Lord spoke to Solomon,

> *"...I have given you a wise and understanding heart, so that there has not been anyone like you before you, nor shall any like you arise after you..."* **I Kings 3:12**

With this supernatural wisdom Solomon spoke three thousand proverbs. Many of these proverbs were concerning relationships within the family. Here are five of those proverbs specifically regarding child discipline.

> *"He who spares his rod hates his son, but he who loves him disciplines him promptly."* **Proverbs 13:24**

> *"Chasten your son while there is hope, and do not set your heart on his destruction."* **Proverbs 19:18**

> *"Foolishness is bound up in the heart of a child; the rod of correction will drive it far from him."* **Proverbs 22:15**

> *"Do not withhold correction from a child, for if you beat him with a rod, he will not die. You shall beat him with a rod, and deliver his soul from hell."* **Proverbs 23:13,14**

> *"The rod and rebuke give wisdom, but a child left to himself brings shame to his mother... Correct your son, and he will give you rest; yes, he will give delight to your soul."* **Proverbs 29:15,17**

Temple of Glory

The family unit has undergone incredible ideological changes in our modern society. One of the main areas of pendulum-like-change has been in the parent-child relationship model. In just a few short years there have been shifts ranging from severely strict discipline to permissiveness which allowed the child to mark on walls with crayons as a means of expressing himself. It's as if family life has been on a trial and error roller coaster. Society ultimately paid the price for these uncertain ideologies: Rebellious, undisciplined children turned into rebellious, undisciplined adults.

There never has been a need to adopt a trial-and-error model as the means to discipline our children. Solomon, given wisdom by God on a scale there never has been nor ever shall be another man with such wisdom, has already given a simple understanding for successful parent-child relationships. ***He told us the proper basis to relate to our children was one of love.*** Even though love is often a very subjective and impractical thing, Solomon showed us very objective and practical applications in parent-child relationships.

By inspiration from the wisdom of God Solomon said foolishness was bound up in the heart of the child, but love will cause a parent to correct his child for foolish acts by applying the rod. Solomon said further that discipline would cause the child to give the parents rest and be a delight to their souls. Solomon continued that lack of discipline was demonstration of parental hate for their child and could cause the child to bring shame to the family unit and ultimately die.

PARENT-CHILD

PARENT-CHILD RELATIONSHIP MODEL

God's parent-child relationship model can be simply organized for clear understanding and practical application. The model has two main components: A parent part and a child part.

Child Part:

According to God's model, foolishness is bound in the heart of a child which causes the child to do foolish things. This foolishness will bring shame to the family unit, cause unrest within the family, cause the child to ultimately die, and not go away of its own accord.

Parent Part:

The parent is confronted with numerous choices in the parent-child relationship, but all of them revolve around only two choices: to love or to hate the child. God's use of this term *"...love..."* more clearly defines relationship than the way we use the term today. For example, today we say, *"...I love junk food..."*; or *"...I love my new car..."* or *"...I love God..."*. Our use of the term *"...love..."* today generally does not accurately identify the type of relationship we mean. When God inspired the term to be spoken by Solomon, it clearly identified the proper relationship as God's-kind-of-love. The kind of love a father is designed to have for his son.

Both choices, love or hate, have practical applications in the parent-child relationship. If the parent spares the rod, withholding correction when the child does foolishly, then according to God, our Father, the parent has chosen *"...to hate his child..."*. If parents knew these two choices were God's perspective, they would not willfully withhold correction. Why is withholding correction from a foolish acting child considered *"...hate..."* for the child in God's sight? Because foolishness left alone in a child's life will cause the child to ultimately die. If you could do something to save your child's life, but you did not do it, God sees that as hate for your child.

If the parent chooses to love the child, he will chasten the child often whenever the child does foolishly. This chastening is a sound application of the rod to the child's bottom so the child cries, not physically abusing the child, but a spanking so the child knows he has been spanked. This action, done in faith and in love, will drive foolishness out of the child, give the child wisdom, and save the child's life.

NATURAL versus SPIRITUAL CORRECTION

In the church today we see many of the same characteristics in Christians as we see in naughty, undisciplined children: rebellious, unruly, non-submissive, out-of-order and uncommitted. These characteristics produce strife in the church which opens the door to every evil working. We can effectively deal with these issues by applying God's model for successful natural parent-child relationships.

The body of Christ is a spiritual family as much as a natural family is a family. Every born-again believer, the instant he is born again, becomes a son with God as his Father. Several New Testament writers have written about the believer in various stages of spiritual growth, ranging from newly born again to mature believers. Peter called the person just born again a babe-in-Christ. He said the babe should desire the milk of the Word in order to grow. This growth out of infancy means the babe will grow through stages similar in comparison to the natural child. God's plan for His sons to receive effective parenting through this process involved parent-child relationships. God's natural parent-child-relationship model as revealed through Solomon can be applied to spiritual parent-child relationships.

Just as the natural parent-child relationship model had two components, so too, the spiritual parent-child relationship model has the same two components: A child part and a parent part.

Spiritual Child Part:

Foolishness is bound in the heart of a natural child. Does this apply to the spiritual child? We do not want to open a theological debate here about whether a born again believer can have "...foolishness..." in his heart. Without considering the theological implications of this matter, there is one thing upon which agreement will be easy to achieve, believers do foolish things occasionally. This foolishness will often bring shame to the local assembly of which the believer is a part, can cause unrest within the church, and will not go away of its own accord.

When a believer is first born again, he is a babe-in-Christ. He does not know the ways of the kingdom of which he has been made a part, which exists in the spirit realm. He finds himself once again having to go through a process of growth, parallel to the one through which he has already grown in the natural world. Just as the person needed parenting to successfully navigate the process of natural growth, so too, the believer needs parenting to successfully navigate the process of spiritual growth.

Spiritual Parent Part:

The spiritual parent, just as the natural parent, is confronted with numerous choices in his parental role, all of which revolve around only two choices: to love or to hate the child. Just as for the natural parent, both choices, love or hate, have practical applications in the spiritual parent-child relationship. Practical application of these two choices focus on discipline. If the parent uses the rod of correction on a foolish acting child, the parent loves the child. If the parent withholds the rod of correction from a foolish acting child, the parent hates the child. These truths are the wisdom of God.

Rod of correction! Is this spiritual parent supposed to make a natural rod and physically apply it to his spiritual children? Of course not! Spiritual parenting deals with the spirit of man, not the natural part of man. The foolish acts of a babe-in-Christ are manifest through the natural man, but the babe needs spiritual correction. Paul told Timothy,

> *"All Scripture is given by inspiration of God, and is profitable for doctrine, for reproof, for correction, for instruction in righteousness, that the man of God may be complete, thoroughly equipped for every good work."*
> **II Timothy 3:16,17**

Limiting use of the Word to doctrine and instruction in righteousness only will create discipline problems within the church on the earth. The Word is equally to be used *"...for reproof and for correction..."*. Many of the *"...negative..."* characteristics of the contemporary church of today are a direct result of an omission of *"...discipline..."*. The church on the earth is a family comprised of sons of God ranging in levels of growth from babe to mature. Wherever there are children, spiritual or natural, there must be discipline. Undisciplined children are rebellious, unruly, non-submissive, out-of-order, and uncommitted, producing strife which opens the door to every evil working.

LIMITATIONS OF PARENTAL RESPONSIBILITY

It has already been established that God is the only *"...true..."* spiritual parent to His sons. It is also already established that parenting responsibilities can be extended through mature believers and those called and or appointed to positions of leadership to lead the sons of God. It is imperative that we consider the limitations of parental responsibility and authority placed on each level of spiritual parenting. It is accurate understanding of these limitations which gives the family of God the potential to operate without strife.

In the natural family the parenting process can involve older brothers and sisters, relatives, or non-family members, as we have already considered. Levels of responsibility for training and disciplining the children within a particular family are set by the *"...true..."* parents. For example, older brothers and sisters are generally not allowed to *"...spank..."* their younger brothers and sisters.

In the spiritual family God the Father determines the levels of responsibility for training and disciplining the spiritual children. The level of responsibility increases through the various levels of maturity, appointment, and calling. Jesus established a principle able to be applied to many things in His church. This principle can be applied to the subject of training and disciplining spiritual children.

> *"...And that servant who knew his master's will, and did not prepare himself or do according to his will, shall be beaten with many stripes. But he who did not know, yet committed things deserving of stripes, shall be beaten with few. For everyone to whom much is given, from him much will be required; and to whom much has been committed, of him they will ask the more."*
> **Luke 12:47,48**

Those called to the five offices of ministry have been given ministry responsibilities and authority uniquely identifying them from other members of the church. The authority and responsibility of the ministry gifts is greater than that of saints who are not called to the five offices of ministry. If all saints had the same ministry responsibility and authority as the five offices, there would not have been grounds for Christ to have given the five offices of ministry. And yet the Holy Spirit inspired Paul to write that,

> *"...God has appointed these in the church: first apostles, second prophets, third teachers, after that miracles, then*

PARENT-CHILD

gifts of healings, helps, administrations, varieties of tongues. Are all apostles? Are all prophets? Are all teachers?..." **I Corinthians 12:28,29**

We see this type of separation of ministry responsibility and authority illustrated throughout the New Testament.

In the early days of the church the dispute among Grecian and Hebrew widows over the daily distribution brought to light separation of responsibilities and authority between deacons and apostles. The apostles declared their primary responsibilities were to pray and minister the Word. By inspiration of God through the apostles' authority, deacons were appointed over the natural distribution of daily goods to the widows of the church. Clearly, responsibility and authority is distributed differently here: The apostles were to minister the Word and pray; the deacons were to distribute natural goods to the widows.

Paul gave Timothy and Titus a list of qualifications to meet when looking for candidates to appoint as *"...elders..."*. Not every Christian could be an elder. Each Christian must meet certain qualifications before being considered for the office of elder. After a believer met the qualifications, had been chosen, and had been appointed to be an elder, then he was uniquely identified among the saints as *"...elder..."*. After being chosen and appointed, the new elder was given specific responsibilities and corresponding authority to fulfill those responsibilities. His choosing, appointment, responsibility, and authority distinguished him from other believers not chosen or appointed.

The separation of a believer into a position of elder does not move him into an *"...elite..."* position better than other believers, but rather, gives him more responsibility to serve the church. Of course, along with more responsibility comes more authority to be able to carry out the new responsibilities.

Because the elder is an *"...appointed..."* position in the church, even though appointed by man called by God, the level of responsibility and authority will not be the same as one of the five offices of ministry *"...called..."* by God. The person called by God will have greater responsibility and authority than a person appointed by man. Understanding this layering effect of diversity, limitation of responsibilities, and authority gives us the basis to function in relation to one another without strife, each uniquely responsible for his own part.

CORRECTING A SINNING CHRISTIAN

The need to help a fellow Christian involved in sin is a standard to which Jesus expects every single believer to adhere. Luke record the words of Jesus addressing this particular matter.

> *"Take heed to yourselves, If your brother sins against you, rebuke him; and if he repents, forgive him. And if he sins against you seven times in a day, and seven times in a day returns to you, saying, 'I repent,' you shall forgive him."* **Luke 17:3,4**

Matthew also records Jesus speaking about this issue. Matthew's account includes an amplification which adds a great deal to our understanding.

> *"Moreover, if your brother sins against you, go and tell him his fault between you and him alone. If he hears*

PARENT-CHILD

you, you have gained your brother. But if he will not hear, take with you one or two more, that by the mouth of two or three witnesses every word may be established. And if he refuses to hear them, tell it to the church. But if he refuses even to hear the church, let him be to you like a heathen and a tax collector." **Matthew 18:15-17**

Every single believer has the responsibility to correct another believer who has sinned against them. This is absolutely not an option if we are going to walk as Christians on the earth. Because this is not an option but rather a requirement, it is necessary to consider the process very carefully. The church on the earth must pioneer restoration of this back into the church. The enemy has surely stolen it from us.

STEP ONE...

Firstly, there must actually be some sin one believer has committed against another believer. There must be great care taken to make certain the infraction is actually a sin and not merely an aggravation of the soul.

My wife and I were members of **Wycliffe Bible Translators** living in Papua New Guinea as translation personnel. We lived in a primitive tribal village the majority of our time in the field. Occasionally, we came together in one setting with other members of Wycliffe to conduct corporate meetings and consider Wycliffe business for life in the field.

During one of these corporate gatherings it was necessary for us to live with another couple for almost one month. I clashed with one of the persons of the couple. Finally, I could not take the conflict any longer. I decided to go to the person, who was a Christian, and confront them with their sin against me. I reviewed **Luke 17:3,4** and **Matthew 18:15-20**, and then communed with the Lord in the matter. I told Him what I intended to do according to His will written in His Word.

He said, *"Fine, that is what I expect you to do if your fellow Christian sins against you."* I felt so good the Lord was agreeing with my decision. Then He asked, *"By the way, what exactly is the sin the person has committed against you?"* I thought, but could not answer the Lord specifically. I was stunned. Before, I was certain the person's actions toward me were sin because they were so aggravating to me. When confronted with specifically identifying the sin, I could not really call the person's actions sin. The Christian's actions and personality were just aggravating to my soul.

Sin committed by one Christian against another Christian requiring correction must be very clearly defined as sin. Sin is a definite violation of the known will of God. Church discipline correcting a sinning believer is for dealing with sin, not personality clashes. And further, most certainly more importantly, dealing with a sinning brother is to help the sinning brother go free of the captivity caused by his sin, not to make the sinned against brother feel better.

If there has been a violation of the known will of God by one Christian against his fellow Christian, the Christian who has been sinned against must go to the Christian who has sinned against him and tell him specifically how he has violated the will of God against him. If the sinning brother repents, then the brother who has been sinned against is to forgive him, and their relationship will be restored. If the sinning brother does not repent, the brother who has been sinned against, with forgiveness in his heart, holds that forgiveness and takes step two in trying to restore the sinning brother and their relationship. It is vitally important to restore a brother and the relationship that is broken because of sin. Paul wrote,

> *"...the wages of sin is death..."* **Romans 6:23**

So long as the Christian has unrepentant and unforgiven sin abiding in his life, he has opened the door for a measure of death to operate in his life. Since we are all members of one body, the body of Christ, if one member of the body has sin and death working in his life, then we are all affected. Paul wrote,

> *"...if one member suffers, all the members suffer with it; or if one member is honored, all the members rejoice with it..."* **I Corinthians 12:26**

If a believer sins and refuses to repent in order to be eligible to receive forgiveness, then he is actively involved in unrighteousness and darkness. This is certainly why Christ Jesus Himself as *"...righteousness and light..."* gave us instructions for dealing with sin in the body.

STEP TWO...

In step two the sinned-against believer goes to one or two fellow believers and tells them the situation. Together they go to the sinning brother and confront him a second time with his sin. ***It must be absolutely clear to all persons involved, the purpose for confronting the sinning brother is to help him be freed from his captivity caused by his sin, not to make the sinned against brother feel better.*** If he repents, forgiveness is *"...extended..."* and restoration takes place. If he refuses to repent, his sin and his actions are to be told to the local church of which they are all a part. This does not mean to make an announcement at the next church service about the sinning brother's sin. Everything must be done decently and in order with restoration as the goal. Rather, they go to the church leadership and share the details of the situation up to its present stage. The sinning brother is once again confronted, this time by the church leadership. If he repents, then the sinned-against believer extends forgiveness and restoration takes place. If he still refuses to repent, then serious action is to be taken in the matter. He is to be exposed to the entire local assembly so that all may treat him as a heathen and a publican. In order to fulfill this ordinance, we must know what the scripture says about how to treat a heathen and a publican.

STEP THREE...

Two key scriptures needed to serve as foundation for understanding this ordinance are written by Paul under the inspiration of God the Holy Spirit. The first says,

PARENT-CHILD

> *"Do not be unequally yoked together with unbelievers. For what fellowship has righteousness with lawlessness? And what communion has light with darkness? And what accord has Christ with Belial? Or what part has a believer with an unbeliever? And what agreement has the temple of God with idols? For you are the temple of the living God. As God has said: "I will dwell in them and walk among them. I will be their God, and they shall be My people. Therefore "Come out from among them and be separate, says the Lord. Do not touch what is unclean, and I will receive you. I will be a Father to you, and you shall be My sons and daughters, says the Lord Almighty."* **II Corinthians 6:14-18**

Historical record has shown this portion of scripture to have inspired cities and communes to have been built by Christians who believe they are conforming to scripture by coming out from among the ungodly. However, that is not the purpose of this scripture. Christians are to be the salt of the earth, the light of the world, and a city set on a hill. Jesus prayed to the Father these wonderful words,

> *"I do not pray that You should take them out of the world, but that You should keep them from the evil one."*
> **John 17:15**

Our God does not want us to move physically away from the ungodly and build separate Christian cities or communes. How then would they see the light? Rather, our God desires us to live next door to them and shine brightly before them. What He does not want us to do is fellowship in their unrighteousness or commune in their darkness. He does not want us to have part in their ungodliness. Paul wrote to the church at Rome,

Temple of Glory

> *"I beseech you therefore, brethren, by the mercies of God, that you present your bodies a living sacrifice, holy, acceptable to God, which is your reasonable service. And do not be conformed to this world, but be transformed by the renewing of your mind, that you may prove what is that good and acceptable and perfect will of God."* **Romans 12:1,2**

In other words, we do not go have a few beers in the local tavern and tell a few dirty jokes to help us win our unsaved friends to the Lord. It is the light which will cause them to be saved, not our identification or conformity to their unrighteous dark ways. Christians are to live and work among the unsaved of the world, but be so separate as the light in our righteous ways, the world can see the obvious difference. Christians are to shun fellowship with unrighteousness just as the light shuns the darkness. Light and darkness are incompatible. They cannot both function successfully in the same room.

The second key scripture says,

> *"I wrote to you in my epistle not to keep company with sexually immoral people. Yet I certainly did not mean with the sexually immoral people of this world, or with the covetous, or extortioners, or idolaters, since then you would need to go out of the world. But now I have written to you not to keep company with anyone named a brother, who is sexually immoral, or covetous, or an idolater, or a reviler, or a drunkard, or an extortioner, not even to eat with such a person. For what have I to do with judging those also who are outside? Do you not judge those who are inside? But those who are outside God judges. Therefore put away from yourselves the evil person."* **I Corinthians 5:9-13**

PARENT-CHILD

The Christian who willfully lives in sin or who has committed sin and refuses to repent after being confronted with his sin is to be treated like the unsaved. We are to live and work around him but as the light in our righteous ways. We are to be so separate from him the world can see the obvious difference. Christ will not have us fellowship with unrighteousness or commune with darkness, even unrighteous acts of darkness in the life of a Christian.

This entire process of correction must be done in the spirit of meekness. Under the old covenant correction was severe, done according to the letter of the law. In the dispensation of the new covenant, correction is in the spirit, not the letter. The sinning Christian is a member of the same body of which we are members. Our interaction is to produce repentance and restoration, not condemnation and guilt. Paul said it this way,

> *"Brethren, if a man is overtaken in any trespass, you who are spiritual restore such a one in a spirit of gentleness, considering yourself lest you also be tempted."*
> **Galatians 6:1**

Areas of responsibilities involving reproof and correction for sin are limited for the babe in Christ to correcting a brother who has sinned against them personally. All believers are to participate in this form of confronting sin. However, even this area of confronting sin will involve elders and or the five-fold ministry if the sinning brother refuses to repent.

PRIMARY REPROOF AND CORRECTION

The primary responsibility for reproof and correction resides with the five offices of ministry and the elders. We see this implied, spoken of directly, and demonstrated repeatedly in scripture. Paul and Peter both charged elders within the church with similar words.

> *"From Miletus he (Paul) sent to Ephesus and called for the elders of the church... ...take heed to yourselves and to all the flock, among which the Holy Spirit has made you overseer, to shepherd the church of God which He purchased with His own blood."* **Acts 20:17,28**

> *"Shepherd the flock of God which is among you, serving as overseers, not by compulsion but willingly, not for dishonest gain but eagerly; nor as being lords over those entrusted to you, but being examples to the flock..."*
> **II Peter 5:2,3**

For the elders to have the *"...oversight..."* of the flock implied they also had reproof, correction responsibilities, and authority. It would be difficult, if not impossible, to have the responsibility to oversee people without also having the authority to correct them.

Paul spoke directly to this matter in his charge to Timothy.

> *"I charge you, therefore before God and the Lord Jesus Christ, who will judge the living and the dead at His appearing and His kingdom: Preach the word! Be ready in season and out of season. Convince, rebuke, exhort, with all longsuffering and teaching."* **II Timothy 4:1,2**

PARENT-CHILD

Paul demonstrated his parental role everywhere he traveled. This role was especially visible in reproving and correcting the Corinthians as Paul even referred to them as *"...my beloved sons..."* (see ***I Corinthians 4:14***). In the dispute over circumcision in the early church recorded in the fifteenth chapter of Acts, the apostles and elders were the ones to make the correction to the Gentile believers.

Are there other areas of correction needed other than that of individual believers sinning against one another? The concept of in-principle will apply here as we have used this concept in other considerations. Reproof and correction are needed from two different perspectives: From the perspective of the word, such as it is written; and from the perspective of the spirit, such as the spirit of a matter. Such reproof and correction is needed regarding two different realms: the natural realm and the spiritual realm. These parameters could easily be diagrammed to make it simpler to understand.

		REPROOF AND CORRECTION	
		WORD	*SPIRIT*
REALM	*SPIRITUAL*	Section One	Section Two
	NATURAL	Section Three	Section Four

Temple of Glory

SECTION ONE:

It Is Written Regarding Spiritual Realm

Correction in this section deals with what is written in the word. Division in the church is anathema to our God. Where such exists, correction is essential in order to restore unity. In the church at Antioch great division arose among the Christians over the issue of circumcision. The church chose Paul, Barnabas, and certain other disciples to go to Jerusalem for help the issue was so divisive.

> *"Therefore, when Paul and Barnabas had no small dissension and dispute with them, they determined that Paul and Barnabas and certain others of them should go up to Jerusalem, to the apostles and elders, about this question."* **Acts 15:2**

Even in Jerusalem there was much disputing over the matter. Then James spoke out saying,

> *"Men and brethren, listen to me: Simon has declared how God at the first visited the Gentiles to take out of them a people for His name. And with this the words of the prophets agree, just as it is written: 'After this I will return and will rebuild the tabernacle of David, which has fallen down; I will rebuild its ruins, and I will set it up; So that the rest of mankind may seek the Lord, even all the Gentiles who are called by My name, says the Lord who does all these things."* **Acts 15:13-17**

Based on James' input showing how God Himself was taking the Gentiles out to be a people to His name, this divisive matter was settled and correction was sent to the church at Antioch. Here the apostles and elders used scripture from the prophets as a basis for correction to Jewish and Gentile believers alike over a very divisive issue.

Another illustration of correction regarding the spiritual realm according to the word can be seen in Paul's letter to the church at Galatia. The Galatian believers were trying to live their Christian lives according to the law. Paul reproved them with correction directly from the word.

> "O foolish Galatians! Who has bewitched you that you should not obey the truth, before whose eyes Jesus Christ was clearly portrayed among you as crucified? This only I want to learn from you: Did you receive the Spirit by the works of the law, or by the hearing of faith? Are you so foolish? Having begun in the Spirit, are you now being made perfect by the flesh? Have you suffered so many things in vain, if indeed it was in vain? Therefore He who supplies the Spirit to you and works miracles among you, does He do it by the works of the law, or by the hearing of faith? Just as Abraham believed God, and it was accounted to him for righteousness. Therefore know that only those who are of faith are sons of Abraham. And the Scripture, foreseeing that God would justify the Gentiles by faith, preached the gospel to Abraham beforehand, saying, "In you all the nations shall be blessed." So then those who are of faith are blessed with believing Abraham. For as many as are of the works of the law are under the curse; for it is written, "cursed is everyone who does not continue in all things which are written in the book of the law, to do them." But that no one is justified by the law in the sight of God is evident, for "the just shall live by faith." Yet the law is not of faith, but the man who does them shall live by them." Christ has redeemed us from the curse for us (for it is written, "Cursed is everyone who hangs on a tree"), that

> *the blessing of Abraham might come upon the Gentiles in Christ Jesus, that we might receive the promise of the Spirit through faith."* **Galatians 3:1-14**

Not only did Paul use the terms *"...it is written..."* and *"...the scripture..."*, but also quoted scriptures to make this correction.

Paul was able to successfully correct the church by comparing New Testament believers' faith with the faith of Abraham, and using the word not only as the standard for correction, but also as the rod of correction.

SECTION TWO:

The Spirit of a Matter Regarding Spiritual Realm

Correction in this section deals with the spirit of a matter, rather than what is written in the word. The incident with Ananias and Sapphira is a good example.

> *"But a certain man named Ananias, with Sapphira his wife, sold a possession. And he kept back part of the proceeds, his wife also being aware of it, and brought a certain part and laid it at the apostles' feet. But Peter said, "Ananias, why has Satan filled your heart to lie to the Holy Spirit and keep back part of the price of the land for yourself? While it remained, was it not your own? And after it was sold, was it not in your own control? Why have you conceived this thing in your heart? You have not lied to men but to God."* **Acts 5:1-4**

Peter did not confront Ananias with what was written in Scripture. Rather, by the Spirit of God, he saw the heart of Ananias and Sapphira and reproved them accordingly.

A similar incident can be found in the eighth chapter of Acts. It will help further our understanding regarding correction in this section. Simon, who had been a sorcerer in Samaria, but who was now born again, saw that the Holy Ghost was given by the laying on of Peter and John's hands.

> *"And when Simon saw that through the laying on of the apostles' hands the Holy Spirit was given, he offered them money, saying, "Give me this power also, that anyone on whom I lay hands may receive the Holy Spirit." But Peter said to him, "Your money perish with you, because you thought that the gift of God could be purchased with money! You have neither part nor portion in this matter, for your heart is not right in the sight of God. Repent therefore of this your wickedness, and pray God if perhaps the thought of your heart may be forgiven you. For I see that you are poisoned by bitterness and bound by iniquity."*
>
> ***Acts 8:18-23***

In this particular illustration it was a combination of Simon who had been a sorcerer revealing his heart by what he spoke out of his own mouth, and the Holy Spirit revealing the poison of bitterness and binding by iniquity that wrought this correction.

Section One and **Section Two** provide clear illustrations of two different types of correction regarding the spiritual realm. Correction in **Section One** was based directly on *"...it is written..."*. Correction in **Section Two** was based directly on *"...the spirit of the matter..."*. Even though correction in **Section Two** was not directly based on *"...it is written..."*, the word was still the standard for the corrections. It was not Peter's own reasoning or words which corrected Ananias and Sapphira or Simon of

Samaria. It was the word of God, Christ Jesus who was the standard for correction. Christ Jesus is the standard for all aspects of life in the church. The Holy Spirit helped Peter maintain this standard by energizing his words with the very life of God to provide reproof and correction.

SECTION THREE:

It Is Written Regarding Natural Realm

The contrast between *Section One* and *Section Three* is merely the realm for which the violation of *"...it is written..."* applies. *Section Three* deals with matters regarding the natural realm such as civil disputes between Christians.

In the church at Corinth certain believers had disputes which arose concerning the natural issues of life. It happened that in some of these cases brother would take brother to court for the case to be tried before a non-Christian judge. Paul brought reproof and correction to the church from his understanding of the Word. The Holy Spirit inspired Paul to write this understanding down to serve as scripture for our future reference.

> *"Dare any of you, having a matter against another, go to law before the unrighteous, and not before the saints? Do you not know that the saints will judge the world? And if the world will be judged by you, are you unworthy to judge the smallest matters? Do you not know that we shall judge angels? How much more, things that pertain to this life?"* **I Corinthians 6:1-3**

PARENT-CHILD

This scripture is saying *"...it is written..."* to correct the natural matter of one believer taking another believer to court before a non-Christian judge over some natural issue of life.

Another illustration of this same type of correction can be seen in Paul's instructions to Timothy as a leader in the church regarding widows and marriage.

> *"Do not let a widow under sixty years old be taken into the number, and not unless she has been the wife of one man, well reported for good works: if she has brought up children, if she has lodged strangers, if she has washed the saints' feet, if she has relieved the afflicted, if she has diligently followed every good work. But refuse the younger widows; for when they have begun to grow wanton against Christ, they desire to marry, having condemnation because they have cast off their first faith. And besides they learn to be idle, wandering about from house to house, and not only idle but also gossips and busybodies, saying things which they ought not. Therefore I desire that the younger widows marry, bear children, manage the house, give no opportunity to the adversary to speak reproachfully. For some have already turned aside after Satan."* **I Timothy 5:9-15**

Paul wrote also to the church at Corinth about this same matter.

> *"But I say to the unmarried and to the widows: It is good for them if they remain even as I am; but if they cannot exercise self-control, let them marry. For it is better to marry than to burn with passion."* **I Corinthians 7:8,9**

This scripture is saying *"...it is written..."* not to take a widow under sixty years, and that the younger widows should remarry because they are not likely to be able to contain themselves.

SECTION FOUR:

The Spirit of a Matter Regarding Natural

The contrast between **Section Two** and **Section Four** like the contrast between **Section One** and **Section Three** is merely the realm in which the violation of *"...the spirit of a matter..."* occurs. **Section Two** involves spiritual matters such as lying to the Holy Ghost. **Section Four** involves natural matters such as interpersonal relationships between saints.

> *"My brethren, do not hold the faith of our Lord Jesus Christ, the Lord of glory, with partiality. For if there should come into your assembly a man with gold rings, in fine apparel, and there should also come in a poor man in filthy clothes, and you pay attention to the one wearing the fine clothes and say to him, "You sit here in a good place," and say to the poor man, "You stand there," or, "Sit here at my footstool," have you not shown partiality among yourselves, and become judges with evil thoughts?"* **James 2:1-4**

James was not establishing seating arrangements in our auditoriums.. Rather he was, by inspiration of the Holy Spirit, illustrating what is to be the proper attitude of our heart toward one another in natural matters. Reproof and correction is to be given to saints if the attitude of their heart is wrong in the sight of God because they give preferential treatment to one above another as a result of external natural factors.

Paul wrote of this same type of issue to the church at Corinth discussing eating of meat offered to idols. He wrote,

> "...food does not commend us to God; for neither if we eat are we the better, nor if we do not eat are we the worse. But beware lest somehow this liberty of yours become a stumbling block to those who are weak."
> **I Corinthians 8:8,9**

If a believer sits down to eat a certain meat knowing it is going to offend his brother who is observing his eating, then he is to be corrected, not because of the meat, but because of the attitude of his heart. His correction is not because he violated scripture about eating certain meats but because he violated the conscience of his brother through his natural eating. Paul said it this way,

> "All things are lawful for me, but all things are not helpful. All things are lawful for me, but I will not be brought under the power of any." **I Corinthians 6:12**

Section Three and **Section Four** provide clear illustrations of two different types of correction regarding the natural realm: Correction in **Section Three** based directly on *"...it is written..."*. Correction in **Section Four** based on dealing with the *"...spirit of a matter..."*. Christ as the Word is the standard for Christian life regarding natural matters just as He is regarding spiritual matters. Reproof and correction can be seen in the natural realm just as in the spiritual realm from two different perspectives of *"...it is written..."* and *"...the spirit of the matter..."*, both with the Word as the standard for correction and as the rod of correction.

In the kingdom of God, whether doctrine and instruction in righteousness or reproof and correction, in order for ministry of the word to produce life, it must be done in the spirit and in love. In the history of the church we have seen even the doctrine of salvation by grace through faith reduced to the letter in some settings *(the Crusades)*. All ministry must be done in the spirit by the power of the Holy Spirit in order to produce life. Reproof and correction are no exceptions.

We have seen simple, clear, and understandable in-principle guidelines for reproof and correction. Yet if they are put into operation in the flesh or power of the soul, they will not produce blessing, but rather bondage. Reproof and correction are needed in the church because we are designed to be a family with many sons and daughters. However, our life in this family must be maintained in the same fashion it began, in the spirit.

We must apply the wisdom of God in our spiritual family setting in order to flourish. In His wisdom He is the only true spiritual parent for all believers in the church. In order for His children to receive parenting according to His plan, He has ordained parent-child relationships between saints. As the true parent, God alone establishes the boundaries for responsibilities and authority in these parent-child relationships. If we can understand these boundaries and operate within their framework, we will begin to see discipline and unity increased in the church. It is absolutely essential that we hold constantly before us that all forms of ministry, all responsibilities, and all authority must be done...

> *"...serving as overseers, not by compulsion but willingly, not for dishonest gain but eagerly; nor as being lords over those entrusted to you, but being examples to the flock..."* ***I Peter 5:2,3***

Conclusion
SUMMARY

God has a plan for man! Not only does He have a plan, He also has a method to achieve His plan. If we can understand His plan and implement His method, then we will see great increase in all of our lives and ministries.

SUMMARY

In summary... God created the earth to be inhabited. Among the inhabitants of the earth man was the center of creation, made in God's own image. God's desire was for man to walk in a relationship of love, sonship, and dominion with Him. Even though the first Adam failed, God's plan for man never changed. God sent Jesus as the last Adam to restore man back to a relationship of love, sonship, and dominion with God.

When God the Father sent Jesus into the earth, the commission He gave His son was more comprehensive than for Him to shed His blood as the price of redemption for all mankind. The Father commissioned Jesus as the man called The Branch to *"...build the Temple of the Lord..."*. This unfulfilled commission is also the commission of the church as the flesh and bone body of the Christ.

In order for Jesus and His body to successfully fulfill this commission, the church must...

1. ...*understand the commission,*

2. ...*have supernatural personnel with divinely given abilities,*

3. ...*have adequate provision of material and funds.*

The commission to build the Temple of the Lord is the most comprehensive building project ever undertaken. It involves all mankind who has in the past or who will in the future respond to the call to salvation. Every individual who accepts the call becomes a temple of the Lord the moment he believes and is born again. As temples each believer must undergo construction to be perfected into the image of Christ. Not only is each believer a temple of the Lord, they are each also living stones. As living stones each must be fitly joined together to form the corporate Temple. Building the Temple of the Lord, individually and corporately, is the commission of Christ and His body!

Every member of Christ's body is a supernatural part designed to help fulflill the commission. However, God has given, through Christ Jesus, supernatural personnel to oversee the perfecting of the saints and the building of the Temple. The supernatural personnel needed to oversee successful fulfillment of the commission are apostles, prophets, evangelists, pastors, and teachers.

CONCLUSION

God supplies each individual believer's need according to His riches in glory by Christ Jesus. He then asks each individual to be responsible for funding His work on the earth. Just as we saw the unchanging God ask the Israelites to be responsible to fund the building of the tabernacle in Moses' commission, this same God has asked the church to be responsible for funding the building of the temple in Jesus' commission. We do not have to give out of necessity or duty, but out of a cheerful glad heart. We can give cheerfully and gladly because our needs have been met supernaturally by God and because we understand fulfillment of the commission will cause God to manifest His life, nature, and ability within and through the Temple to all mankind.

In order to make these requirements for success work, we must focus on individuals in the church. We cannot be so corporate goal minded that we lose sight of the individual's need and value within the church. Each individual's success in Christ bolsters the success of the corporate church.

Success in Christ is not gaining more money, newer cars, bigger houses, and nicer clothes, which is how the world views success. These may be by-products of our success in Christ but not success itself. Success in Christ from God's perspective is:

> 1. Each individual believer developing an intimate relationship with God so he is established in righteousness, peace, and joy.

2. Because of this relationship with God, each believer will have the supernatural ability to walk like Christ.

There are four components necessary to cause individual Christians to become a success in Christ.

1. Input from the five-fold ministry...

...each office planting seeds according to the perspective of their calling. Just as it takes input from both the father and the mother to present a complete picture of natural life to the children of a family, so too, it takes input from all five offices of ministry to present a complete picture of Christ to the family of God.

2. Active Involvement of the Holy Spirit's ministry in the life of every individual believer...

...activated by the faith of the believer so the *"...seeds..."* of the word can be transformed into living revelation of the Christ, which is personal relationship with Jesus.

3. Each person in the church asking, seeking, and knocking...

...involved in a quest to know God.

4. Every member of the body of Christ set into the church as it pleases the Father, and functioning as God designed them to function...

CONCLUSION

...joined together with other living stones in a local assembly in practical, living, daily relationships. It is when we are *"...joined..."* together that His life has freedom to flow through us supplying nourishment from every part so the body can make increase of itself in love.

Finally, in order for us to mature as God intends, we must see the scripture restored to a place of use for more than just doctrine and instruction in righteousness. We must see reproof and correction revived in the church. This is designed to be done through proper application of God's parent-child relationship model between the saints.

www.ingramcontent.com/pod-product-compliance
Lightning Source LLC
Chambersburg PA
CBHW061641040426
42446CB00010B/1525